CHINATOWN, U. S. A.

by Calvin Lee

CHINATOWN, U.S.A.
CHINESE COOKING FOR AMERICAN KITCHENS

CHINATOWN, U. S. A.

CALVIN LEE

1965
DOUBLEDAY & COMPANY, INC., GARDEN CITY, NEW YORK

TO BEVERLY

Acknowledgments

The author is indebted to hundreds of people for their assistance in writing this book. Elliot Schryver is responsible initially for the idea of the book and following through for several years tirelessly with editorial advice, encouragement, and constant nagging until the manuscript was completed. The author interviewed hundreds of people throughout Chinatown, U.S.A., and while it would be impossible to thank all of them the following should be thanked especially for sharing with the author their insight on the Chinese in various parts of America: K. L. Lee, Berne Lee, Sam Choy, Sunny Pang, Honorable Thomas Tang, Reverend Lawrence Stanley, Walter Ong, Mr. and Mrs. Harry Ginn, Albert Gee, Dr. and Mrs. Colin Dong, Dr. T. D. Lee, Liem Tuai, Herbert Mark, Soleng Tom, Mrs. Esther Tom, Mrs. Theodore Wu, Jerry Lee, Mr. and Mrs. Lo Yi Chan, and Mr. and Mrs. Ned Chou. Mr. Yook Ou very generously shared his extensive and carefully compiled bibliography on the early history of the Chinese in America. The research of the subject was greatly facilitated with the help of Mr. Thomas Ai of the China Institute of America and the librarians at the California Historical Society and Columbia University. Many friends made helpful suggestions including Mrs. Ann Sparks, Mr. and Mrs. David Edwards, and Mr. and Mrs. Edward Bernath. Mrs. Ann Dickstein and Mrs. Kay Howell not only typed the many drafts of this book, but offered many helpful suggestions in the process. Robert Ballou's editorial criticism helped the author to tie up loose ends. Finally the author is indebted to his wife, Beverly, who helped with the interviews, criticized various drafts, contributed many insights, kept our children quiet and was a constant source of moral support.

Calvin Lee

Contents

List of Illustrations

Introduction

Chinatown, U.S.A., is to most Americans the most distant country in their midst. It is a curiosity, a place to sight-see, a wonderful place to eat and to purchase objects of art and handicraft. For me, who grew up in New York's Chinatown, it was, and is, something else. I do not find it easy to describe my "hometown" as a special kind of place. I did not realize until I had become an adult and had moved away from Chinatown that I had grown up in a carnival atmosphere in which thousands of visitors come to see sights.

Don't expect me to create for you the mysterious and sinister atmosphere of Chinatown which Hollywood has portrayed, because it never existed. But ask me about what makes Chinatown "tick"—the people—and I think that you will be in for an interesting story.

Among the American beliefs about the Chinese in the past are the following: They are a mysterious and in-scrutable race and do everything backwards. All Chinese are honest and absolutely trustworthy. They are all cunning and crafty. The Chinese never lose their tempers. All Chinese look alike. They never say what they mean. Chop suey and chow mein are their national dishes and besides these dishes they eat nothing but rice. Their favorite delicacies are rats and snakes. A Chinese is properly a "Chinaman" and the word "Chinee" is singular for "Chinese." A "Chinaman" never gets drunk. The Chinese are a nation of laundrymen with a highly developed civilization. The Chinese invented pretty nearly everything that was ever invented.

The image of the Chinese in America is a combination
of stereotypes created by the early newspapers and magazines, and later added to by Hollywood. From 1920 to
1930 there was the image of Fu Manchu, evil and inscrutable. Later, when there was an era of good feeling
toward the Chinese, the image was of that of Charlie
Chan, clever and patient. The advent of Communist
China may have the effect of changing the image again
to the evil and the inscrutable. Such a notion is utterly
strange to the second, third, and fourth generation Chinese-Americans. We are entering the professions and we
feel as American as ham and eggs. Some of our friends
of American ancestry are amazed at how little many of
us know about China and Chinese culture. Most Americans know no Chinese except the neighborhood restaurantmen and laundrymen, who have established the everyday view of us. Many Chinese-Americans try to rub out
this image. Many are defensive about it. Actually, thousands of Chinese in America are intellectuals and university students stranded here because of conditions in
China. They are careful to differentiate themselves from
the "lowly" Chinese restaurantmen and laundrymen. Yet
the latter, these humble hard-working people, through
their quiet, patient and honest ways, have created the
true image of the Chinese-American as an honest and
peaceful people. It is to these people that this book is
dedicated in the hope that it may help Americans to
understand them.

If one ever looks at the listing of the department of
Chinese in the Columbia University catalog, he will find
the "Dean Lung Professor of Chinese" which was established in 1902 by General Horace W. Carpenter. Dean
Lung was the name of the man who for many years was
General Carpenter's Chinese butler. After many years of
loyal service, General Carpenter asked Mr. Lung what
he could do for him in recognition of his work. Dean

Lung asked the general if he could do something to en-
able Americans to learn something about Chinese culture
and philosophy. General Carpenter made a very large
contribution to Columbia to establish a Chinese department and a library. Dean Lung himself donated his
entire life savings of $12,000. It has become one of the
finest Chinese departments in America and has made a
tremendous contribution to the understanding of Chinese
philosophy and culture.

It is to people such as General Carpenter's Chinese
butler, the early miners, railroad builders, laundrymen,
and restaurantmen that we owe gratitude for sitting it
out through thick and thin and creating that fascinating
country within a country—Chinatown, U.S.A.

CHAPTER 1

Land of the Golden Mountains

The old-timers in Chinatown seldom, if ever, speak about the colorful days of their youth when they first landed. When they reminisce, they talk about the old country, the hamlets and villages where they were born. They seldom speak of the hard times they have lived through here. Never will they speak of the prejudices from which they have suffered. If they seem inscrutable, if they do not become involved in the affairs of the town, it is because of the haunting troubles of the past. Those early days of the Chinese in this country tell a great deal about why there are so many Chinese laundries and restaurants, and why there are Chinatowns.

The formal name of America in Chinese is *Mei Kwok*, "Beautiful Land," but colloquially the Chinese still refer to America as *Gum San*, the "Land of the Golden Mountains," a name given by the first groups of Chinese coming to America to discover gold in the early 1850s. Just when the Chinese first reached America nobody knows. It may have been before the days of the Clipper ships and the China trade of the nineteenth century. Some archaeologists accept the Chinese symbols which are part of the lore and dress of the Mexicans as evidence of early contact with North America.

Perhaps the Chinese cabinboy of the *Bolivar* who is said to have reached California in 1838 was the first of his race to reach America. Or were the two Chinese men and one woman whom Mr. Charles V. Gillespie, a New York merchant, and his wife brought in with a cargo of goods from Hong Kong in 1840 the first? A colorful tale is that of Madam Ah Toy who some say was the first Chinese woman to arrive in San Francisco. There are two versions of the Ah Toy story. In one she was a woman of high caste and intellect who entertained politicians and churchmen at her tea parties. In the other, she lived in a shanty in a blind alley just off Clay Street and displayed herself in her pantaloons of willow green silk to miners for an ounce of gold a "look" until some miners started to cheat her by leaving brass filings.

Some say that Chum Ming, an enterprising man who sold tea, shawls, and other Chinese goods before he took to the hills for gold in 1847, was the person who wrote to Canton about the discovery of gold and thus started the Chinese emigration to California. The news spread in China that high wages were being paid to laborers, and circulars printed and distributed by brokers of foreign shipmasters advertised that the cost of the trip would be only $15. (Later it rose to $50.) This fare to California was three to five times less for the Chinese immigrant than for the European. Placards, maps, and pamphlets pictured the Land of the Golden Mountains as a place of heaven. In 1850 forty-five vessels left Hong Kong for California with nearly five hundred passengers packed like cargo into the holds of the ships without fresh air or sunlight for the long journey across the Pacific. By the end of 1851 there were 25,000 in California.

Droughts in China from 1847–50 caused a great crop failure in Canton Province, driving many overseas. Other immigrants during the early period left China for political reasons. The Triad Society and other secret orders opposed to the Manchu Dynasty seized upon the time that the government was engaged in combating the Tai Ping Rebellion in the north to instigate an insurrection. These orders were subdued with much bloodshed, and thousands of the rebels sought refuge in America. Furthermore, after the British defeated the Chinese in the first Opium War (1839–42) unemployment hit the port of Canton due to the Nanking Treaty which opened ports in Shanghai, Ming-Po, Amoy, and Foochow. The reason for Chinese emigration during this early period was not much different from that which brought the Irish and German agricultural immigrants to the port of New York at the same time. However, there was a difference between the purposes of the two groups. Most of the Irish and German arrivals came to stay. The Chinese, on the other hand, were sojourners—*gum san hoch*. Most were married men who had come to America only to earn enough money to buy land in China to which they planned to return. Some were only recently married, an arrangement made by their parents to insure their return. In the first two decades, about half of them returned to China, but thereafter, at least in the opinion of the Caucasians on the West Coast, too few returned and too many kept coming.

The Land of the Golden Mountains lived up to its name for some early Chinese. At Moore's Flat in the Yuba River district, two Chinese found a 240-pound nugget of gold worth over $30,000 which had been kicked about and overlooked by white miners. Some others working on a deserted claim at the middle fork of the Feather River found a 40-pound nugget and quietly chiseled it up into small pieces and sold it with their other gold dust, avoiding excitement and the possibility of the nugget's being reclaimed by the original mine owners.

During the early 1850s the vices of gambling and opium which the Chinese brought with them were not as offensive as their hoarding of gold. Almost all the gold which they found was sent to China. Their financial contribution to the economy of California was almost nil since the only purchases which they made were fresh meat, flour, and a few other foods. There is some evidence that they first adopted American clothes but later changed back to their native costumes except for heavy mining boots. The editor of the *Oriental* on February 15, 1855, pointed out that changing back to native costumes was one of the reasons for the anti-Chinese attitude among the Americans. The editor suggested that his countrymen wear American clothes and become westernized in order to prevent friction with Americans.

Almost every mining town had its Chinatown with its Chinese placer miners, its prospectors, its merchants, as well as its launderers and cooks. One of the largest exclusively Chinese mining camps, still called "Chinese Camp," was located a few miles south of the mining town of Sonora, where there were reportedly over 20,000 Chinese.

Chinese began to work in the mines in force in 1851. The *Daily Alta California,* on April 10, 1852, wrote:

A very large party of Celestials attracted considerable attention yesterday evening, while passing down Washington Street, on their way to the southern mines. They numbered about 50, each one carrying a pole, to which was attached large rolls of matting, mining tools and provisions. . . . They appeared to be in excellent spirits and in great hopes of success, judging from their appearance. They are but the vanguard of a few regiments that are now on their way here from the celestial empire.

On May 3, 1852, the *Daily Alta California* said:

For the last few days our streets have swarmed with Chinese, on their way to the southern mines. Day after day dray-loads of shovels, picks, pans, matting, rockers, and provisions followed by a drove of chattering Celestials, have passed down the streets on their way to try their fortunes in the mines. Nearly all are encased in strong water-proof cow-hide boots, some with red shirts, and one of the gang risked the reputation of his personal appearance by wearing an old shovel hat, apparently made for a monk of the 14th century. The low price of passage to Stockton tends to draw them all towards the southern mines, as the cheapness of traveling is a stronger argument to persuade them in what direction they should go than any other that might be adduced. The southern country will soon be alive with them whether their advent prove beneficial or not.

The larger Chinese settlements were in Nevada City, Auburn, Coloma, Placersville, Angeles Camp, Chinese Camp, Coulterville, and Hornitos. Among the early settlements, Sacramento was the communication center of the mining regions. It is called "Second Port of the Golden Hills," the first being, of course, San Francisco, and Marysville the "Third Port of the Golden Hills."

The peaceful engagement of Chinese in gold mining was very short-lived. One of the reasons for the sudden anti-Chinese feeling was the sudden unprecedented immigration in 1852 of 18,400. A mass meeting was held in the Columbia mining district on May 8, 1852, condemning certain shipowners, capitalists and merchants from flooding the mines with "the long-tailed, horned and cloven-hoofed inhabitants of the infernal regions." Chinese miners were driven away from mining districts of the Sierra Nevadas, Marysville, and Horseshoe Bar. White miners of Weber County burned the tents and mining equipment of Chinese miners and turned back stage coaches carrying Chinese passengers. The cry, made up mostly of Caucasian immigrants, was "California for Americans" and the movement was to get rid of the "Yellow Peril."

In many communities, posted notices ordered them out

of the district. The following posted in Mariposa and other towns in the Agna Fria Creek district in 1856 is typical:

Notice is hereby given to all Chinese on the Agna Fria and its tributaries, to leave within 10 days, from this date, and any failing to comply shall be subjected to 39 lashes and moved by the force of arms.

Only rarely did one hear of any concern for the rights of Chinese. The citizens of Butte County pursued four white men who escaped from the sheriff and hanged them after they had confessed to murdering a Chinese man. There was little other news of this kind in that day.

At first only the miners among the Chinese were expelled, but soon thereafter the discrimination spread to merchants and laborers in the towns as well. In the Agna Fria Creek district, property owners were urged not to rent or renew leases to Chinese under the pretext that the Chinese quarter was a fire hazard: the Chinese used fire in open pans instead of stoves for their cooking and they shot off firecrackers on their feast days and were continually burning punk sticks before their religious images.

A Foreign Miner's License tax was passed to exclude the Mexicans from the mines. It was used almost entirely against the Chinese, produced an income of more than $5,000,000 between 1850 and 1870, and was collected from all Chinese whether or not they were miners.

The collectors of the tax roamed over the mining districts acting so outrageously that it spurred the *Nevada Journal* to say:

There is a species of semi-legalized robbery perpetrated upon the Chinese. Many of the collectors are gentlemen in every sense of the word: but there are others who take advantage of their position to extort the last dollar from the poverty-stricken Chinese. They date licenses back, exact pay in some instances for extra trouble in hunting up the terrified and flying Chinaman, and, by various devices fatten themselves upon the spoils thus obtained. The complaints of the injured and oppressed find no open ear, for is it not declared by the Supreme Court, the highest tribunal in the Land, that their oaths are not to be regarded? Of what avail are their complaints, uttered not with the solemnity of an oath? Under this state of things the life of a Chinaman in California is one of hardship and oppression.

It was not until 1873, when California's Revised Code took effect, that Chinese witnesses were admitted into evidence in the courts. When the Chinese first arrived in California, Indians and Negroes could not testify. When the question of whether Chinese testimony should also be excluded, Chief Justice Murray of the California Supreme Court ruled that the word "Indian" included Mongolian. Judge Murray's opinion which unashamedly included an amazingly ignorant discussion of ethnology arrived at the theory that although the word "Indian," as commonly used, referred only to the North American Indians, yet as in the days of Columbus all shores washed by Chinese waters were called the Indies, therefore all Asiatics were Indians.

At every turn the Chinese were squeezed by taxes or licenses. As early as 1852 the California legislature passed a law which was a thinly disguised "head tax." The law required all masters of vessels to post a $500 bond for each alien passenger in order to indemnify the state against medical costs. As an alternative the bond could be commuted by a payment of not less than $5 nor more than $10 per passenger. The income was to be distributed among the state's principal hospitals. The income from this tax through the years amounted to over

$400,000 of which the Chinese paid never less than 45 percent and in 1869 as much as 85 percent. The benefits, if any, of this scheme, however, never accrued to the Chinese since they were excluded from the city hospitals in San Francisco. The law was finally declared unconstitutional. The "Police Tax" passed in 1862 was another "head tax" designed for Mongolians who had not paid the Miner's Tax. This fortunately was declared unconstitutional in the next year by the California Supreme Court.

The gold rush for the Chinese was extremely brief. Taxes, licenses, and persecution drove them away from the rich mines. Some remained in placer mining of "spent" and deserted mines, being satisfied with not more than five or six dollars a day as opposed to fifty or sixty. Others, however, sought new means of making a living.

Some settled along the coast and prospered as commercial fishermen. The catching and exporting of abalone to China became profitable but in 1860 a tax of $4 per month was imposed on all Chinese engaged in fishing. However, the revenue from this tax was so small that the law was repealed in 1864. A law regulating the size of small meshed shrimp nets used chiefly by the Chinese was passed upon the complaint of the Italians and Greeks who were in the fishing industry. Of the 2500 fishermen in the San Francisco area in 1893, one-quarter were Chinese.

No one realized at the time, and few remember now, that Chinese labor in California during this early period developed the resources of the state as they would not have been developed otherwise. California was dependent upon the East for her manufactured goods and supplies which could not be delivered cheaply and quickly. She had land but had not irrigated it or cultivated it. She had the perfect weather for growing fruit but she did not have the human resources to plant it, care for it, gather it, and build a transportation system to bring it to market.

The end of gold mining did not end the lure of the "Golden Mountains." Steamers kept coming into the wharfs of the Golden Gate with even greater numbers of Chinese. They came now not to dig for gold but to "rent strength."

CHAPTER 2

Crocker's Pets

The word "coolie" was a synonym for Chinese labor, implying servitude, peonage, even slavery. Supposedly introduced into China by Englishmen, the word came from the original Bengalese or Tamil word *kuli* meaning burden-bearer. In Chinese the term "coolie" is two words, the first *koo* meaning to hire or to rent and the second *lee* meaning strength. To the Chinese the expression meant to "rent strength"—to hire out or to do unskilled labor.

At that time unskilled labor sent to Cuba, South America, and British Guinea for a term of service was held in semi-slavery. Though considered by many in the same way, the Chinese immigrants to California were voluntary, many of them selling what little property they had to pay for passage across the Pacific. The poorer ones borrowed at exorbitant interest rates, very often using a relative, particularly daughters, for collateral.

The notion that the coolies were not free men rose from the sight of hordes of Chinese arriving at the port of San Francisco with passage prepaid. They were met at the port by representatives of the Chinese Six Companies, or associations, transported as a group in carts to Chinatown and there assigned jobs by agents who seemed to make all the arrangements for them. It was, of course, believed by the prejudiced lower white class that these coolies were imported by the Chinese Six Companies who held them in servitude. Thousands of Chinese who worked for the Central Pacific Railroad signed promissory notes for passage, but this was deducted from their wages in the first seven months on the job after which they were completely free. They were not much different from the indentured servant of the early colonial days.

The Chinese Six Companies were associated in a federation, first of six, later of seven, district organizations consisting of Ning-Yeung Company, Hop-Wo Company, Kong-Chow Company, Sam Up Company, Yang Wo Company, Yan-Wo Company, and the Shen Hing Company. Each of these companies represented a geographic district of Canton Province from which almost all of the Chinese immigrants came. The word "company" was used not to mean a business organization, but to designate an association or group. They were not different from a Texas Club or Brooklyn Club for people far away from home. Since the spoken dialects of the various districts were different, the immigrants clustered in groups of those from the same home areas. They came at first in small numbers, and as they became successful in America, they wrote back to China about their good fortune and encouraged others from their districts to join them. Soon these informal district clubs had small buildings and meeting halls in San Francisco to coordinate the matters of the immigrants in America.

At first, they could best be described as travelers' aid organizations helping the immigrant find a place to sleep until he could find employment. Following the custom at home where the elders arbitrated all disputes between members of a family, these district companies, particularly as the Chinese could not use the courts in America, took on the responsibility of arbitration between its members. When the disputes were between members of different districts, the federation of the Six Companies had to take over.

While the early immigrants were, so to speak, indepen-

dent entrepreneurs in gold mining and in their own
businesses, the Six Companies could remain simply a
travelers' aid. As the demand in California for unskilled
labor rose, the Six Companies began to function also as
employment agencies. As American companies started
to ask for labor in the hundreds, then thousands, the individual associations could not fill the orders and consequently had to join forces.

Hundreds of Chinese arrived at the wharfs of San
Francisco. As they filed out of the ships they separated
into district groups. Uniformly dressed in blue cotton
shirts and pants, according to Chinese style, they were
received in express wagons at the docks by the representatives of the district associations. For the first time in
over forty days, they could breathe fresh air and stretch
their legs. Before they had a chance to admire the
Golden Gate, they piled their few belongings onto the
wagons and trotted alongside or behind them until they
reached Chinatown. By the mid 1850s a Chinese settlement had already grown up on DuPont Street in San
Francisco. In Chinatown the new immigrants were tem-
porarily housed and fed at the district meeting halls or
with friends while the organizations found jobs for them.

As the number of Chinese immigrants grew, the animosity toward them also grew and soon they could depend on a welcome of rocks and bricks from howling and
screaming white hoodlums. The regular police could not
or would not do anything about it. A group of white
citizens organized a "Chinese Protective Society," which
lasted for only one year, and spent several thousand
dollars for a special police force to protect these newcomers from the Orient.

To the immigrant, this strange new country offered a
means of support not only for himself but for the large
number of relatives he left behind. His responsibility was
not just to his wife and children but to his parents, broth-

ers and sisters, grandparents, nephews and nieces. His list of dependents would seldom have less than five names on it, and often as many as twenty. He came from an agricultural society where for many generations his family had tilled a small piece of farmland, scarcely enough to feed the family. His only hope of improvement was to leave his village, earn money outside and purchase land. Unskilled and unread, he had only his strength to offer. Whatever hard work lay before him, it had to be done to fulfill his obligations as a good son, husband, father, or brother. To white employers he seemed fatalistic, willing to take on any dangerous task or excruciating burden for a small wage. But, to him, there was nothing fatalistic about it. It was the only hope of salvation for his family; to turn back without success would have meant losing face with his entire family.

The sense of filial piety was an ingrained attitude. It was, and had become, the backbone of the social structure and social order of the village societies from which these people came. It was not, in most cases, something which they learned from books. Perhaps few had ever heard of the *Book of Filial Piety,* yet even those who could not read and write were taught respect for their elders as part of the great teachings of Confucius, who had edited the ancient classic.

The strong family feeling and solidarity was important to the agricultural society. Survival depended on unity rather than individuality and on males rather than females. It is clear that boys were preferred to girls.

Viewed in these terms, it is not surprising to find that very few women immigrated to America during this early period. (The same was true of the early immigrants from Italy.) The man emigrated to the foreign country in order to make a living (and hoping to make a fortune) for his family (which included his relatives). There was no purpose in bringing his wife. Her job was to raise the children already born, and care for her mother-in-law. Besides, it was an expensive trip. The wife also served as the "lure" or "bait" to make sure that the man came back home.

Individual happiness had no room in this kind of social structure, the success of which depended upon each member discharging his responsibility to his group, rather than seeking the satisfaction of his own desires. It is perhaps the biggest point of disagreement between American-born Chinese and their China-born parents or grandparents.

To the white employers the Chinese were a godsend. All the employer had to do was to engage a crew of laborers through one of the associations in Chinatown. Each labor group had a spokesman who handled all problems and needs, housed them, fed them, and guided them for a dollar a day per person. Soon the vineyards of Southern California were filled with Chinese laborers who plowed, irrigated, planted, picked, and dried fruit. They filled the swamps and reclaimed the marshes. They were vegetable gardeners on plantations on the Sacramento River. They could be found in lumber camps, paper and powder mills, tanneries, tin shops, and factories. Three large woolen mills in San Francisco claimed that they could not operate without Chinese labor. There were over seventy establishments run by Chinese for the manufacture of boots and shoes. In 1862, 90 percent of the cigars and cigarettes sold on the Pacific coast were made by Chinese.

Some of the immigrants established their own businesses. The *Daily Alta California* reported in 1850:

> Much excitement was caused in the city last week by the reduction of washing prices from $8.00 to $5.00 a dozen. There is now no excuse for citizens to wear soiled or colored shirts. The affect of the reduction is manifest—tobacco juice bespattered bosoms are no longer the fashion.

At one time laundry had to be sent to Canton or Ho-
nolulu. Before the Chinese came, laundry was done by
Spanish-American and Indian women who washed on the
borders of a little fresh-water lake about two miles from
San Francisco. Wah Lee started the first Chinese laundry on Washington Street. By 1876 San Francisco had
three hundred Chinese laundries each employing about
five men. What the first Chinese laundrymen, farmers by
trade, knew about washing and ironing, heaven only
knows! What they did know was that the regular price
was $8 for doing a dozen shirts, that there were very
few women in California to do this kind of work, and
that at $5 a dozen they, the Chinese, could get the busi-
ness.

To economize on rent, two firms would very often use
the same premises alternating night and day around the
clock. The laundrymen who followed the gold miners to
the West were able to pan soapsuds and find gold dust
from dirty shirts, a bonus added to the regular price for
laundry. In 1869, a Mr. Thomas of New Jersey hired
fifty Chinese to work for his large laundering concern.
Soon there were Chinese laundries throughout the country.

The old Chinese laundryman of that era sprayed shirts
from a mouthful of water, ironed night and day with a
heavy iron, and was the subject of ridicule and curiosity
in the town. He tried to buy the goodwill of children
with lychee nuts, but the stories of a large chopping
knife hidden under the counter was ingrained into young
minds and the image of an opium-smoking rat-eating
"Chinaman" stuck. Today the laundry business is quite
different.

For the early laundry pioneer in a city or town where
few other Chinese lived, there could not have been a
more lonesome existence. He worked and lived by himself; he was unable to communicate with Americans; he
could only dream of retirement back home.

Other individual entrepreneurs were the vegetable
vendors who went from door to door with a basket on
each end of a shoulder pole and the door to door "chair
fix 'em man." Probably the one who did most to further
understanding between Americans and the Chinese was
the Chinese houseboy. He was able to command twice
as much in wages as the Irish hired girl. Compared to
the life of the laundryman or the laborer, the houseboy
had the advantage of being able to live, at least vicar-
iously, a full and pleasant family life. He became a part
of the family, raised the children, cooked the meals, did
all the shopping and shared in the happiness and sorrows
of the family. And he was found in almost every well-
to-do home in California in the last half of the nineteenth
century.

In a somewhat different, but no less important, cate-
gory were "Crocker's Pets."

When the "Big Four," Charles Crocker, Collis P. Hun-
tington, Leland Stanford, and Mark Hopkins, took on the
assignment of building a railroad from the West Coast
to the East, they had no idea that they were going to
affect the history of immigration in America. In 1863
when the Central Pacific was started there were sufficient
Irish and Mexican laborers. But Irishmen left the jobs
to look for easier work as soon as they had money in
their pockets. Mexicans never overcame their dislike for
this type of strenuous work. Thus, Crocker and his part-
ners were stuck with the almost impossible task of building a railroad across the Sierras where the problems of
terrain and climate were insurmountable.

Stanford and E. B. Crocker, Charles' brother, peti-
tioned the War Department to send five thousand rebel
prisoners to be put to work, but before anything came
of that the Civil War ended. A plan of importing, under
contract, thousands of peons from Sonora and other Mex-

ican states never got beyond the discussion stage because the experience with Mexican labor had been poor.

The idea of using Chinese may have been suggested by Charles Crocker's servant Ah Ling. It seemed preposterous to employ such "fragile" people, only five feet tall and with an average weight of 110 pounds, to do the heavy work of blasting and pickaxing through the Sierra Mountains. No one thought of how the Chinese had built the Great Wall of China. Crocker was desperate and sent for fifty Chinese laborers. At the end of the first twelve hours of work, all doubts vanished and the search for Chinese railroad workers began. Within six months Crocker had two thousand Chinese working for $40 a month and the work was going at a great pace. The white laborers called them "Crocker's Pets" and Stanford felt obliged to write long company reports defending the practice of employing Chinese labor.

The demand was so great that thousands of Chinese had to be imported directly from China. Their passage was prepaid by the railroad and each of the laborers signed a promissory note for $75, which was to be repaid in seven monthly installments from the wage of $40 per month. The story is that "Cholly Clockah" paid his men personally. Once a month he would ride into camp with two large saddlebags, gold in one and silver in the other, call off the payroll one by one, and drop the coins into the outstretched hands.

The upper American River Canyon was swarming with six thousand of "Crocker's Pets" by the summer of 1866. While hundreds of the men chiseled away to make cuts in the rock, others, in a long human chain, carried away the debris in wheelbarrows. The graders were followed by the track-layers and a never-ending line of men. The most difficult bit of track-laying in 1866 was at Cape Horn Mountain which offered no footholds in its thousand-foot vertical sides of granite. Workers had to be low-

ered from the top precariously in baskets and suspended
in the air while the first ledges were made with hammer
and chisel. Then the ledges were widened to permit
the laying of track. The next difficulty came at Cisco,
ninety-four miles from Sacramento, where the granite
was so hard that even blasting powder was ineffective.
It was here that the engineers started to use something
that they were still not familiar with—nitroglycerin. Sum-
mit Tunnel, a one-quarter-mile bore through hard granite, took one whole year. The project was plagued with
frequent accidents from nitroglycerin explosions. Not
only did the work proceed from both ends, but a shaft
was made from above so that men could also work outward from the middle thus attacking the rock on four
fronts. Even with twelve-hour shifts they could not bore
more than eight inches a day.

The winter of 1866 brought continual snow and sub-
zero weather and it was almost impossible to get any
work done with the ground frozen and the tracks covered
with great drifts. Only in the tunnels and deep cuts could
construction work be carried on. Almost half of the men
were needed to help clear the line of snow, and by January it was impossible to maintain paths from the lines
to the camps. For the rest of the winter, the men went
to work through tunnels dug underneath snowdrifts forty
feet deep. This eerie existence was complicated by the
constant danger of avalanches. On at least four occasions
an entire camp went hurtling into a canyon, killing a
number of workmen, to be buried there until spring.

Finally, in June 1868, Crocker's men reached the Nevada state line and the Central Pacific Railroad had completed the most difficult part of its project. From this
point on, the object was to try to beat its competitor,
the Union Pacific, coming from the East, in the number
of miles of tracks laid. The race was on with Chinese
laborers building toward the east and the Irish toward

the west. In fact, the two crews laid tracks right past each other and for miles the lines paralleled but refused to join. Major General Grenville M. Dodge, the head of the Union Pacific team, said:

"Between Ogden and Promontory, each company graded a line running side by side, and in some places one line was right above the other. The laborers upon the Central Pacific were Chinamen, while ours were Irishmen, and there was much ill-feeling between them. Our Irishmen were in the habit of firing their blasts in the cuts without giving warning to the Chinamen on the Central Pacific working right above them. From this cause several Chinamen were severely hurt. Complaint was made to me by the Central Pacific people. One day, the Chinamen, appreciating the situation put in what is called a 'grave' on their work, and when the Irishmen right under them were all at work, let go their blast and buried several of our men. This brought about a truce at once. From that time, the Irish laborers showed due respect for the Chinamen, and there was no further trouble."

The point of joining the rails, however, had to be fought out in Washington, and it was finally selected as Promontory Point, six miles west of Ogden, Utah, and by the end of April 1869 the seven-year job drew toward its close and almost ten thousand Chinese laborers were finished with their work.

CHAPTER 3

"The Chinese Must Go"

Charles Crocker had predicted that when the railroad was completed the Chinese would return to China. Instead, more came. From 1851 to 1860, 61,397 were admitted to the United States. From 1861 to 1870, 64,301 were admitted, and from 1871 to 1880 the figure jumped to 123,201. Toward the end of the 1870s the demand for Chinese labor declined. The railroads had been built, five-and-one-half-million acres of swampland in California had been reclaimed. The industries which were needed on the West Coast had been developed. The mines had been opened.

The attempt to use the Chinese as a scapegoat in politics was tried as early as 1852 by California's Governor John Bigler. The rise of the Know-Nothing Party, whose purpose was to exclude all foreign-born from holding office and to discourage immigration, gave a new impetus to the anti-Chinese movement in California. On the Atlantic coast, the Know-Nothings clamored against the Irish-Catholic immigration; on the Pacific coast, the Irish-Catholics and other European aliens practiced racial prejudice against the Chinese. While the politicians were preoccupied by the Civil War and Reconstruction, while the white aliens were still preoccupied with the fast-made fortunes which could be found in mining, and while the railroads were employing nearly 10,000 Chinese, the anti-Chinese agitation could not crystallize. By the end of the 1870s the economic boom of the Pacific coast came to an end. In August 1875, the Bank of California had to close its doors. The period of quick money from mining had ended, and the white laborers had to turn to regular work. Some of these white immigrants were the strong and the adventurous who had no intention of working for wages. Their failure to make a fortune in the West and their consequent bitterness, made them anti-railroad, anti-corporation, anti-capital, all of which was rolled into anti-Chinese slogans. They organized trade unions and as early at 1867 their influence could be felt by the political parties. Denis Kearney became one of the most influential anti-Chinese agitators and held nightly meetings at a place called the Sandlot in San Francisco. He gathered the unemployed, the hoodlums and the bums under the banner of "The Chinese Must Go."

A newspaper account dated April 1, 1876, said:

A RIOTOUS ASSEMBLY

An inflammatory Anti-Chinese Meeting was held last evening on Kearney Street, and addressed by an incendiary orator. Under his heated harangue, the crowd was wrought up to the highest pitch of excitement, and increased in numbers until the street was blocked by a surging mass. The speaker read a long series of resolutions condemning the importation of coolies, demanding a remedy from the law-making power, and ended by proclaiming that if no measures were taken to suppress the plague, the people were justified in taking summary vengeance on the Mongolians. The resolutions were received with yells by the listeners, and several unlucky Chinamen who passed by at the moment were knocked down and kicked, to emphasize the verdict. The speaker then resumed his address in a more incendiary strain than before, calling on the populace, in the name of humanity, and their families, and as American citizens, to "drive every greasy-faced coolie from the land." "We must take this insidious monster by the throat" shouted the speaker, "and throttle

it until its heart ceases to beat, and then hurl it into
the sea!" At the conclusion of this speech he called
upon every man to sign the resolutions, which about
two hundred of those present did. During the crowd-
ing up to accomplish this, a car passed along on which
a Chinaman was riding. Yells of "pull him off! Lynch
him! Kill the greasy slave!" etc. rent the air; but the
Mongolian escaped with only a few cuffs and a vigorous kick or two . . .

Riots and assaults upon the Chinese people became so
numerous that the Chinese were advised to keep off the
streets and "out of the sight of Christian men, lest they
be massacred in cold blood."

The newspapers have told how closely the Chinese
followed the advice:

At 9:00 last night, the streets in the Chinese quarter
were almost deserted and nearly all the stores closed.
Special policemen were stationed at each corner, and
the place had decidedly the appearance of a town under martial law.

Shutters were all closed; a great part of the houses
were dark, the streets were entirely deserted by Celestials, and the few people who were passing seemed
for the most part incited by a curiosity to see how the
inhabitants of this quarter were deporting themselves
during the excitement. The hoodlumistic element was
slightly represented, but was restrained from acts and
even words of violence by the presence of the police. . . .

A little back from the entrance of several of the
blind alleys on Jackson Street could be seen, notwith-
standing darkness, the shadowy forms of a few anxious
ones, and an occasional guttural sound caught the ear,
but, probably, never in the last 15 years have the streets
of this part of San Francisco, been so free from Chinamen as they were last evening.

A morning paper said:

It is scarcely safe for a Chinaman to walk the streets in certain parts of this city. When seen, whether by day or night, they are mercilessly pelted with stones by the young scape-graces who now, there being no school, have nothing else to do, while older hoodlums look on approvingly, and, if the Chinamen venture to resist the assaults, take a hand in and assist the youngsters. Chinese wash houses are sacked almost nightly. A Chinaman apparently has no rights which a white hoodlum, big or little, is bound to respect.

Among the favorite targets for arson and robbery were Chinese laundries. Great riots occurred in San Francisco in July 1877. In the first, twenty-five Chinese laundries were burned. Other towns followed the example of the San Francisco rioters. In November 1878, Truckee was in a state of anarchy and a thousand Chinese were driven away.

These riots and disturbances, at first unofficial, became more closely associated with the political parties, and soon the persecution of the Chinese became legal with the new anti-Chinese ordinances. Representatives in San Francisco passed what was known as the Cubic Foot Ordinance. This ordinance provided that sleeping space must allow 500 cubic feet of air for each person. In the first attempt to enforce the ordinance, fifty Chinese were dragged out of their beds from a lodging house which, according to the *Bulletin*, had "about the same air capacity as the forecastle of a coaster." The judge fined them each $10 but under the advice of several Chinese organizations, most of them refused to pay, and were sent to jail. The jails were soon filled to overflowing and the police found themselves the laughingstock of the city. According to the *Bulletin*, "the police are earnestly engaged in mathematical calculation, with plan and diagram to determine about the precise space a Chinaman requires while in the flesh."

As a reprisal the officials passed a new ordinance which required that all prisoners "under conviction should upon arrival at the county jail . . . have the hair of their heads cut off or clipped to a uniform length of one inch from the scalp thereof." This ordinance also backfired as the sheriff was sued for cutting off the queue of Ho Ah Kow. The court sustained Ho's argument. The officials had imposed a degrading and cruel punishment upon a class of people who were entitled with all the other people in the United States to equal protection under the law. Ho's second argument was that the loss of his queue would, according to his religious faith, bring him misfortune and suffering after death. Although accepted by the court, the argument did not have merit because the queue actually had no religious significance. This was an American misconception of which Ho Ah Kow took advantage. Historically it was a badge of submission introduced to China by the Manchus—a custom which was finally discarded only when Dr. Sun Yat-sen formed the first Republic of China in 1912.

The Board of Supervisors of San Francisco re-enacted the laundry ordinance requiring every Chinese laundry-man to pay a license fee of $15 per quarter unless he delivered the laundry by horse and cart, in which case the license fee was $2. At this time Chinese laundry was delivered by men carrying the laundry on shoulder poles. Other arrests were made for discharging firecrackers, carrying vegetable baskets and other technical infractions which were not enforced against any save the Chinese.

The agitation against Chinese labor became more and more effective as the mobs picketed, struck and boycotted manufacturing concerns and other employers of Chinese. Their aim was the discharge of all Chinese labor, regardless of whether the whites were willing to perform such labor. Able to live and eat more cheaply, the Chinese were willing to take lower wages. The strikes by the white laborers ostensibly for higher wages and shorter hours actually were for the removal of Chinese competition. It took the governor and the state militia to stop the riot of three hundred Irish and Italians who struck at the Amador Mine. At the end of the riot the Chinese were fired and wages were slightly increased.

The California Senate made a report on the Chinese situation in California and summed up the objections to the Chinese as follows:

> During their entire settlement in California, they have never adapted themselves to our habits, mode of dress, or our educational system, have never learned the sanctity of an oath, never desired to become citizens, or to perform the duties of citizenship, never discovered the difference between right and wrong, never ceased the worship of their idol gods, or advanced a step beyond the traditions of their native hive. Impregnable to all the influences of our Anglo-Saxon life, they remain the same stolid Asiatics that have floated on the rivers and slaved in the fields of China for thirty centuries of time . . .
> Of all the vast horde not four hundred have been brought to a realization of the truths of Christianity. . . . It is safe to say that where one Chinese soul has been saved . . . a hundred white have been lost by the contamination of their presence.

The influence of this biased committee report was great. In August 1877, more than 10,000 copies were published and distributed to members of Congress, governors of states and newspapers. A special committee of Congress was formed to look into the matter and its point of view was just as bad, if not worse.

In 1877 the Workingman's Party was formally organized and became a serious challenge for both the Republican and Democratic parties. In the California state
legislature of 1879–80 the Workingmen in coalition with
the Grangers and Democrats passed a law making it a
misdemeanor for a corporation to employ Chinese. A
fine of from $100 to $1000 might be imposed for a first
offense, and $500 to $5000 for a second. The law was
declared invalid because it violated the Burlingame
Treaty and the 14th Amendment. Meanwhile in Washington the Fifteen Passengers Bill, which limited each
incoming vessel to fifteen Chinese immigrants, narrowly
passed both houses of Congress and would have become
law were it not for the veto of President Rutherford B.
Hayes who felt that the bill abrogated the Burlingame
Treaty.

The 1868 Burlingame Treaty with China, the first gov-
erning the rights of the Chinese residing or trading in
the United States, guaranteed reciprocally the privilege
of school or colleges, and of residence or travel and guaranteed against persecution on account of religious belief.
It pledged the territorial integrity of China, disavowed
any intention on the part of the United States to inter-
fere with the internal administration or trade of China,
and recognized the right of voluntary emigration making
enforced emigration by the subjects of either power a
penal offense. As a result of agitation and political pres-
sures, the United States entered into another treaty with
China in 1880 stipulating that the "United States may
regulate, limit, or suspend such coming or residence, but
may not absolutely prohibit it. The limitation or suspen-
sion shall be reasonable and shall apply only to Chinese
who may go to the United States as laborers, other
classes not being included in the limitations."

The United States under this treaty agreed to exert
all its power to devise measures for the protection of the

Chinese in the United States and to secure to them the same rights, privileges, immunities and exemptions as may be enjoyed by the citizens or subjects of the most favored nation.

In 1882 the United States passed its first exclusion act prohibiting the entry of Chinese laborers for ten years. In the following years, Chinese exclusion was extended and made harsher by more regulations, restrictions, and by required registration of all Chinese in the United States. Other acts made it impossible for Chinese to become citizens or to bring their wives to the United States. It was not until 1943 that the Congress of the United States repealed the Exclusion Act of 1882, and granted a token annual quota of 105 for persons of Chinese ancestry.

Looking back, one wonders whether history would have been different if more Chinese had accepted Christianity, if fewer of them had clung to their oriental costumes, if they had not been so eager to work for almost any wage, if they had not sent their money home, if they had at least learned to speak English. A combination of events and attitudes made this agitation almost inevitable. The Chinese immigrants were sojourners with no desire to be assimilated by American society at this time. They happened to be in the United States at a period of unrest and economic recession and they became the easy scapegoats. Also, about this time, certain criminal elements in America known as the highbinder tongs controlling prostitution, gambling and opium developed, bringing the Chinese as a race into disrepute until the 1920s.

CHAPTER 4

Chinese Social Structure

An understanding of the Chinatown community requires at least a brief discussion of social structure in China because parts of it were transplanted to America. For centuries there were only two classes. Eighty percent of the population were peasant farmers who lived in the countryside. The other 20 percent of the population formed a mobile upper class consisting of landlords, merchants and minor officials in the towns, the landed-gentry, scholar-literati, successful merchants, militarists, and high officials living within walled cities. The development of Chinese literature, art, philosophy, and ethics came from this upper class and filtered down to the masses, with inevitable modifications.

The immigrants came from the peasant farmer class and their knowledge of Chinese culture and philosophy is the result of this filtering-down process. Because of this it is, of course, different from classical interpretations of Chinese philosophy. The sojourner left behind him a large family living in houses of bamboo or brown sun-dried brick. The powerful family system gave China its strength as well as its inertia. Without ingrained patterns of social behavior, individuals could not have survived the trying vicissitudes of peasant life or sojourner life for that matter. But social stability was accomplished at the expense of progress.

The most important social unit in this society was the family, not the individual or the village or state. It was a patriarchal society with the father ruling over the family, its property, and even the marriages of his children.

Obedience and filial piety were ingrained from childhood and the result was respect for elders. Confucian philosophers have classified family status as composed of the "five relationships" which are those between: ruler and subject, father and son, elder brother and younger brother, husband and wife, and friend and friend. Other kinship relations such as paternal aunts and uncles, maternal aunts and uncles, cousins, grandparents, and in-laws were also appropriately fixed in family status. The burden of head of the family passed from father to eldest son.

The philosophy of status and obedience according to status is an important part of Confucianism. Also associated with Confucianism are those quiet virtues such as patience, reverence for ancestors, the aged and the learned, the golden mean, pacifism and compromise, and humanism. The five Confucian virtues are benevolent love, righteousness, propriety, wisdom, and faithfulness. These are perpetuated by the strong traditional family structure. The immigrants to America brought along with them these attitudes and philosophies which influenced their behavior here. This accounts for their ability to endure the hardships and the loneliness. It gives us an understanding of the social structure in Chinatown which was transplanted here. It also poses a dilemma for the American-born Chinese who have found that the Confucian virtues fortified by family solidarity become a barrier to their development as individuals in American society.

The pattern of behavior in Chinatown is predominately that of village society rather than one born of the more modern and cosmopolitan attitude of coastal cities such as Canton and Shanghai, or Hong Kong. Many of the recent immigrants who spent much of their lives in Hong Kong consider the people in Chinatown old-fashioned.

Large old Chinatowns such as those in New York and
San Francisco particularly are reminiscent of a China
which hasn't existed even in China for twenty years.

The "old world" heritage is reinforced not only through
the teaching of filial piety but also through such social
organizations as clan and family names associations, district and village associations and other China oriented
groups.

The first associations formed were based on geographic origins and called district or village associations. Since a predominant number of the early immigrants came from eight of the ninety districts of the
province of Canton and were recruited from these villages or districts in groups of twenty-five or more at one
time, it was natural that these villagers formed a kind of
camaraderie when they arrived at the shores of the United
States. Nam Hai, Toi Shan, Sun-Wui, Shun Tak, Hai Ping,
Yan Ping, Pun Yui, and Chung Shan were the eight districts which supplied most of the immigrants.

Although the identity or relationship to the village or
district was secondary to clan or family relationship at
home, the fact that the inhabitants of the different districts spoke slightly different dialects and had somewhat
different customs inhibited at first the functioning of the
traditional clan or surname societies. Actually the dialect
of each of these eight districts, though it was not identical with any of the others, was intelligible to all of them.
But the difference was great enough so that one's alle-
giance was at first stronger to the district association than
to someone of the same surname of another village.

The Chinese Six Companies, mentioned earlier, was a
federation of these district associations. It was at one
time a very powerful and respectable organization in the
Chinese community. It was the first pressure group on
behalf of the Chinese in America and hired attorneys
and spokesmen to speak up for the rights of the Chinese.

Unfortunately, the police chiefs in San Francisco assumed it was a criminal tong and weakened it so greatly by discrediting it that it could not efficiently operate on behalf of the Chinese in America. Now called the Chinese Consolidated Benevolent Association, the Chinese Six Companies has evolved into a quasi-judicial superstructure in Chinatown politics. It runs Chinese schools, sometimes oversees business transactions, arbitrates disputes between members of different family associations in a quasi-judicial capacity, and attempts to represent itself as the spokesman for all Chinese.

Clan associations were formed for people of the same surname, i.e., Lee, Wong, Chin. Because they are so far away from home, all persons of the same surname are considered "relatives" and the associations' activities to some extent overlap those of the Six Companies, caring for the aged, widows, and children, acting as employment agencies, settling disputes and sometimes arranging social functions such as those which mark Chinese New Year. The sojourners have attempted to transplant the traditional family social structure by means of family associations. Due respect is given to the opinions of elders until they reach senility at which time their room and board is taken care of through the facilities of the association. Generally once an immigrant has settled here, his loyalties are stronger to the clan association than to the district or other associations. Family association headquarters vary in size from small rooms above a mercantile store to whole buildings in larger cities. The largest of them are equipped with social rooms in which *mah jong* is played. There are kitchen and dining facilities for single men, a meeting room, and dormitories. The secretary or treasurer of the family association handles savings and loans, and writes and reads letters for the illiterate.

Both the district and the family associations have continued to operate as informal employment agencies. Owners of businesses when looking for employees always let their associations know of their needs. New immigrants and unemployed men find jobs by referrals through the associations. This is particularly helpful in smaller towns and cities without Chinatowns where an employer can write to the association of his needs and a prospective employee can be interviewed and put on a train to the city in which his new job is located.

The role of employment agency can be seen in the Tang clan control in Phoenix, and the Lee's activities in Washington and Philadelphia, and the Moy's in Chicago. Among the district associations, the Young Wo clan supplied most of the farmers for the Sacramento Valley. San Yap went into businesses as tailors or merchants and the Sze Yap control most of the laundries, restaurants, and Chinese shops in San Francisco.

The role of the family or district association as an arbiter has been much less effective. The Chinese brought with them a social structure which was basically family oriented and family centered. It was a system based on the leadership of the elders of the clan and its rules of behavior were enforced by social sanctions. The clan council could impose a variety of punishments ranging from a reprimand to removal from the clan rolls. It always involved a loss of "face." While this was effective in small villages in China, and for a number of years in America, the clans today have lost their power of enforcement because social sanctions are not enough.

In recent decades district and clan associations have lost many of their functions. During the depression of the early '30s, these organizations provided relief for their members and an amazingly small number of Chinese applied for welfare at that time. Since then, welfare legislation has taken away the role of the clan association in the care of the aged, widows and children. The one function still very important is furnishing English interpreters to help members apply for social security or state and federal aid. Although the associations still boast of large memberships, their active paid membership represents only a fraction of the members of the district or clan. This is attributed to the great number of Chinese who work outside of Chinatown today and to the fact that American-born Chinese rarely join such organizations. Although clans still arbitrate disputes, it is no longer rare to find Chinese bringing matters before an American court.

Mr. K. L. Lee of Washington, D.C., who served as the Eastern Regional President of the Lee Family Association of America from 1957 to 1961, has tried to rejuvenate the Lee Family Association. Fluent in both English and Chinese, he believes that Chinatown must be preserved as a place for cultural contact and identity particularly for Chinese-Americans. He feels that Chinatowns must be made desirable and attractive places to visit. The image of Chinatown as a place of gambling, opium dens, and tong wars must be destroyed. He believes that a family name association which can get elders to work together with younger Chinese-Americans could accomplish these purposes. Mr. Lee himself has done much to improve the Chinatown of Washington, D.C., where he lives. Through his efforts, the Lee Federal Credit Union was formed under the auspices of the Lee Family Association. He knew that many of the elders had capital which was not even kept in banks and he also saw that many younger educated people needed capital to start new businesses. To convince the older non-English speaking men to deposit their money into a newly formed credit union so that the money could be put into circulation to help the non-Chinese speaking youth was no easy task, nor was it any easier to convince the "Americanized" younger generation that a credit union under the Lee

Family Association would be run democratically and not patriarchally. Some of the Lee Associations have scholarship funds established by the elder and old age funds established by the younger members. It is Mr. Lee's hope that these ideas may sooner or later be copied in other Chinatowns and by other family associations.

It is generally felt by all Chinese-Americans and by many of the business people that the tongs and the Chinese Consolidated Benevolent Association have held back progress. They maintain that the Chinese Consolidated Benevolent Association particularly has too many fund-raising projects for new buildings and Chinese schools and has produced few results. Although these tongs as well as the family and district associations do not have any power to enforce their wishes, they may exercise social ostracism or worse still, business boycott. But, the tongs, family, and clan associations today are given token tribute and lip service. Their real influence, if any, is only on the older Chinese and they have lost their influence almost completely with Chinese-Americans, with the people working outside of Chinatown and even with the more enlightened Chinese businessmen in Chinatown. These organizations represent the last stronghold of conservative Chinese family ties with the old world. Unless they can take on new functions, it is doubtful that they can survive much longer.

Unfortunately one cannot write about Chinatown without saying something about tongs. The word tong in Chinese means a hall or an organization. To the American public the reference is to the criminal tongs, highbinders, and hatchetmen. The American press which seems to love "cops and robbers" took to the romanticized stories of sinister crimes, opium dens, cunning and crafty Chinese, and bloodthirsty "hatchetmen"—*boo tow doy*. On the other hand, in recent years magazine articles and television programs have espoused the theory that the tongs no longer exist and that the Chinese family system has prevented juvenile delinquency. It is unfortunate that the American impression of the Chinese has always swung from one extreme to the other. The record should be set straight.

Tongs still exist as merchants' associations or clubs although there have been no tong wars since the early 1930s. In the eyes of most Chinese people the tongs must still be tolerated, although fear was once prevalent.

The tongs, which started in San Francisco, consist of six major associations. On Leong, Hip Sing, Ying On, Bing Kung, Sui Ying, and Chee Kung (also known as Chinese Masons). As early as 1854 two tongs, the Hip Sing and the less important Kwang Duck, had been organized. Initially they were organized for the purpose of mutual aid and protection but soon they became involved in vice, mainly prostitution and gambling. The Chee Kung Tong, which calls itself the Chinese Freemasons or Masons, began its activities in San Francisco in 1863. It was originally a secret society, known in China as the Triad, dedicated to the overthrow of the Manchu Dynasty, but in the United States it also became involved in various illegal activities.

With a potential membership of thousands of lonely, hard-working Chinese men, it is not surprising that the criminal elements would hit upon the organization of prostitution, gambling, and opium. The demand for women was so great that the kidnaping of Chinese girls in broad daylight became the cause of many tong wars fought mainly by hired gunmen or *boo tow doy*—hatchetmen, so named because of their use of an ax or cleaver as a weapon. The unique style of these hired assassins included the use of *chun hung*, the posters which were placed on the walls in Chinatown offering a reward of several hundred to several thousand dollars for the assassination of an individual.

In 1898 police Lieutenant William Price of San Francisco estimated that there were approximately three thousand so-called "highbinders" in San Francisco. This figure might be close to the total membership of the tongs, which included a good number of businessmen who joined the organizations for self-protection. The number of salaried killers was probably between three and five hundred.

The subject of tongs and tong wars makes up a great part of the lore and legend of American Chinatowns. The most talked-about celebrity of this early era was Fong Ching, alias "Little Pete," who was known as the tong war boss of Chinatown in San Francisco. "Little Pete" was a natural for the sensational journalism of the time. When he was assassinated in a barbershop in 1897 at the youthful age of thirty-four the newspapers told an elaborate tale of his activities. Little Pete arrived in America at the age of ten and worked in a shoe factory. He was ambitious and intelligent and at night he went to school to learn to speak English fluently. With the exception of his dress, which was always the finest of Chinese costumes, he was known as the most Americanized Chinese in the San Francisco of that time. After a few years working in the shoe factory, he managed to save and borrow enough to start his own factory under the trade name of F. C. Peters & Company. He hired white salesmen to deceive his white customers and became wealthy. Not being content with this income, he also ran several gambling dens. Before long he was heading a tong which exacted tribute from various gambling dens in the city. Little Pete in his attempt to free his bodyguard Lee Chuck from a murder charge got himself indicted for attempting to bribe a police officer, who was the state's witness in the case. It took three trials before a jury could agree that he was guilty. After his stay in prison Little Pete returned to his business as usual except that he became interested in horse racing. Soon it developed that he had been winning constantly and was finally thrown off the tracks for bribing jockeys. His last mistake was sending his white bodyguard out on an errand just before he walked into the barbershop unprotected and was shot to death by other tong men for a handsome reward.

In spite of the changing character of the tongs, there is still a strong suspicion that they are paid tribute by gambling houses and other illegal enterprises. The membership of such organizations has greatly declined. Businessmen and family men no longer feel the need to join for protection.

CHAPTER 5

The Chinese People in America

Persons of Chinese ancestry in America can be generally divided into three groups: the sojourners, the Chinese-Americans, and the visiting scholars.

The early Chinese immigrants were almost all sojourners or *gum san hok* (Gold Mountain guests). Until the Communists took over the mainland, most immigrants still so considered themselves. Although they may not have had any definite plans to return to their villages, their mental orientation was that of their home. The object of their hard work in the United States was their enjoyment years later in the villages in which they were born. Living frugally, they sent every cent they could spare home where it was invested usually in land. Since their orientation was toward China, they had no inclination to become Americans. They made no effort, except sometimes for business reasons, (and even then only minimally) to adopt new customs, language, clothes, or food. They insulated themselves from the Caucasians and devoted themselves to achieving social status at home with the sweat of their brows here.

Esteem and honor was not to be measured, in their eyes, by the opinions of Americans. They never looked at themselves as others here saw them, as foreigners. They formed ghettos. The immigration records are not clear at all as to how many Chinese sojourners went home to retire. Certainly less than half. Some went home every five years or so for a visit and returned to America to work again. The goal of all was a fortune large enough to retire on and support a large family. But for many it remained constantly out of reach.

The sojourner's success or failure within the Chinese community both here and at home was measured by how many times he had returned to China. It was a mark of his financial achievement to be able to afford the costly trip and the time away from work. It was important that this first trip home occurred if possible within five, but certainly no later than ten, years after his arrival to indicate the dedication and earnestness he was devoting to his goal. If he had been successful in sending large sums of money home to purchase status symbols such as brick houses, rental property, and other business enterprises his social status at home was made, even though he was at the bottom of the social ladder in America. If he became wealthy enough, he could even make donations to village welfare projects such as schools, temples, and roads and be known as a philanthropist in his small village.

His personal prestige both in his village and in Chinatown rose if his generosity helped kinsmen to come to America so that they could start on their own ladder of success. This nepotism was very common and is the reason why certain families dominate particular Chinatowns. In the city of Phoenix, for instance, almost two-thirds of the Chinese belong to the Tang clan.

On any leisurely evening in Chinatown at a noodle house where the Chinese eat their midnight snacks or perhaps in front of the steps of a store one can overhear the tale of the sojourner's trips home told and retold. On such evenings, the listener, whether he be a relative, employee, or new acquaintance nods attentively to the story which makes life here bearable. On each succeeding trip major events took place. The sojourner would relate, for instance, how on his first trip he brought home many presents to his aging parents and relatives and purchased land. On his second trip he saw his son, who was born

after he had returned to America from the first trip. And
on each succeeding trip there were more children and
more houses and more land. Finally he would talk about
the plans for his final trip home, when he could cease to
be *gum san hok,* a sojourner.

How many successful sojourners reached their hard-
earned goal of retirement in China no one knows. With
mainland China now in Communist hands the sojourner
no longer has a place that he can call home. Many have
reconciled themselves to dying in a foreign land. Some
have become American citizens and started to change
their attitudes.

At the same time that Chinese laborers were coming
to the Land of the Golden Mountains to make a living,
a much smaller group of young Chinese students came
for their education. The person who most influenced this
movement was Yung Wing, who with two other Chinese
boys came in 1847 to study at Monson Academy in Massachusetts. Yung Wing then was graduated from Yale
College (now Yale University) in 1854 and returned to
China to try to convince and recruit Chinese students to
go abroad for Western education. It was a difficult task
to get sponsors for such a project. Why should bright
young intellectuals leave a country with thousands of
years of traditional classical education for education in
a new country that was barely a hundred years old? Finally, in 1872, the Chinese educational mission sent thirty
students to the United States.

Since that time it is estimated that 22,000 visiting Chinese scholars have come to America. Some have remained, particularly after World War II. Of this group
are two Nobel Prize physicists and others making major
contributions.

Until World War II, almost all of these students were
men. The tradition-bound Chinese society even of the

cosmopolitan cities of Peking and Shanghai still felt that the woman's place was in the home.

The Exclusion Act of 1882 and the National Origins Act of 1924 did not exclude visiting scholars who had no intention of remaining in America. After the turn of the century, the value of a Western education became recognized and was important for social and economic status in China.

Until World War II, most of these students did return to China. Under the immigration laws it was very difficult for them to do otherwise. Also their opportunities in China were much greater where the knowledge gained in agriculture, engineering, architecture, and the sciences could be put to practice, often gaining for them high posts in the government or in universities. Most of these students took up some branch of science because this was the most desperate need of China. Few came to study philosophy or the social sciences because it would have been difficult to change the classical education back home. It was not practical.

Those interested in the social sciences, primarily economics and business, did not come in any numbers until the Manchu Dynasty was overthrown in 1912. The classical educational system emphasizing Confucian ethics, the Analects, and rituals ended in 1905. The contribution made by these returning students cannot be measured, but it must have been great. Whereas Western ideas and ideals would have been resisted if given by well-meaning and well-intentioned foreign scholars and missionaries, these Chinese students paved the way for an acceptance of more modern methods of doing things.

One visiting scholar who made a tremendous impact was Dr. Hu Shih, who has been known as the "Father of the Mass Education Movement." A student of John Dewey at Columbia, Dr. Hu Shih revolutionized the Chinese language by getting the scholars, writers, newspa-

pers, and publishers to stop using the very stylized and
ancient forms of writing and adopting "plain language"
which was writing the way one would speak. Hitherto
the form of writing or even a letter or newspaper was so
formal and stylized that even if one could read the ideo-
graphs, he could not understand their meaning. Dr. Sun
Yat-sen, the first president of the Republic of China, was
also a student in America.

For a number of years, Chinese students in America
outnumbered any other single group of foreign students
with the exception perhaps of those from Canada. They
have attended schools in almost every state in the country, showing preference for eastern schools such as Columbia, Harvard, Yale, Princeton, Cornell, the University
of Pennsylvania, and Massachusetts Institute of Technology. The University of Michigan has had a great
number of Chinese foreign students and others such as
Purdue and the universities of Wisconsin and Illinois have
been popular. Later in the twentieth century when the
western states became more established and the unpleasantness of outward anti-Chinese behavior had subsided,
Stanford and the universities of California and Washington have had great numbers of these visiting students.

After World War II the United States sought to help
China's postwar recovery by allowing thousands of Chinese students to come to America for advanced training.
Financial support for the program came from the United
States Technical Assistance Program, the Nationalist government, and scholarship aid from American universities.
But in 1952, the Nationalist government was forced by
economic need to curtail its support. The United States
government, through the Emergency Aid Program of the
Economic Co-operation Administration continued its educational aid until 1955. After the fall of mainland China
to the Communists, some five thousand Chinese students
were stranded in the United States.

Adjustments were difficult. If the Nationalist government had not fallen, they would have been assured a high social and economic status in China, either at a university or in the government service. Here in America, they found themselves in a foreign country, competing with others with Ph.D.s and starting at the bottom of the ladder. If there was no overt racial discrimination, there was at least a more subtle form resulting in the Caucasian getting better jobs, quicker advancement, and greater administrative responsibility than the Chinese. The older visiting professors found it difficult if not impossible to get comparable teaching positions in American universities and had to settle for posts as lecturers or instructors at less than the best institutions.

Because they had been assured of higher status when they returned to China and because of their education, the visiting scholars always were careful to differentiate themselves from the "lower class" Chinese laundrymen and restaurant owners and their children, the second generation Chinese-Americans. The sojourners and American-born Chinese reciprocated by calling the students snobbish spoiled children.

Part of this animosity must be attributed to a difference in language. The laborers and merchants in the United States spoke Cantonese and most of the foreign students spoke the Mandarin of Peking which was not intelligible to the Cantonese, and vice versa, though some of the students were from the province of Canton. Many of these were supported by kinsmen in America. But many were helped by sojourners with food, lodging, and such weekend jobs as waiting on tables. The sojourners, after all, were great admirers of the educated class of scholars, students, and officials which traditionally held the highest positions in China. Through helping these students, they experienced vicarious satisfaction in contributing to

a new China. It also, of course, made them feel superior
to have young intellectuals under them as employees.

Because of the early anti-Chinese movements and the
very low status of Chinese laundrymen and restaurantmen, and the bad publicity brought about by the tong
wars, most of the foreign students, even those from Canton, avoided association with Chinatown. They felt that
their acceptance in American society could only be accomplished by disassociation from this uneducated class
of peasants. This feeling was passed on to their children,
the Chinese-Americans, who were considered by the foreign students as cultural hybrids, neither Chinese nor
American.

Through a twist of fate, a somewhat closer relationship between the Mandarin speaking and the Cantonese
speaking people has resulted. Many Mandarin-speaking
people stranded in the United States have found that the
only places where they can make a living are Chinese
restaurants and curio shops. The increase in the number
of Mandarin-styled, Shanghai-styled, Peking-styled Chinese restaurants has been a direct result of the numbers
of stranded students seeking to make a living here. Because of this, they have had to deal with merchants in
Chinatown who supply them with Chinese groceries and
vegetables. At the same time, the Cantonese merchants
in Chinatown have sought to keep this trade as well as
the retail trade of Mandarin-speaking families buying
supplies for home use by employing Mandarin-speaking
salesmen. Several Chinese grocery stores in Chinatown
have done this and have monopolized the business of the
housewives. You can say, therefore, that the animosity between these two Chinese groups has reached a point of
truce, even if not of friendship.

More than one half of the 240,000 Chinese in the U.S.A.
today are American-born. Most of them are second and
third generation. The second-generation Chinese-Ameri-

can in Chinatown is brought up in an environment which tries to stress Chinese attitudes of filial piety. Until the Sino-Japanese War in the 1930s, many of the American-born Chinese children were sent to school in China during their teens. When they returned after completing high school, they found that they had not sufficient education in either Chinese or English to do anything except to continue in the business in which their parents were. While in China, they had married. When they returned, they brought their wives back with them. Their children, the third generation, received all of their education in America and had become American except for their physical appearance and perhaps some Chinese attitudes regarding respect for elders. Those who were not brought up in Chinatown have probably been completely Americanized.

The second-generation Chinese-Americans who were born in Chinatown and educated in China are a breed of people frustrated in their careers because of an insufficient amount of education in either. My father, who was one of these, used to say, "What good is half a pail of water?" These people, however, have been the bridge which has joined China and America. Although neither sojourner nor American, their orientation for their children has been clear. They have resolved that the American-born would be educated completely in America, but also that they should know how to speak Chinese as well as English, and become acquainted with Chinese customs. Whether they have been successful in the latter has depended largely on whether they have lived in Chinatown or not. If they have moved to the suburbs and have not spoken Chinese at home, the Chinese culture has been completely lost. There are Chinese language schools in every city where the Chinese population is more than one thousand. But this is an uphill disparate battle because the Chinese-American children view a parental order for them to attend such schools as interfering with their attempt to become completely assimilated into American society. They resist any attempt to make them different from their Caucasian classmates. They try to learn just enough Chinese to speak to their foreign-born mothers or grandparents, but their attempt results in a "chop suey" type of dialect with a liberal dose of English thrown in. After a short visit by his grandmother, my four-year-old son announced at dinner that he was going to say "park the car in Chinese." My wife, delighted with this first attempt into bilingualism, listened attentively as my son said, "Parkee car." Poor grandmother, she dies a thousand deaths as she sees in two short generations the complete loss of thousands of years of Chinese tradition. These children don't even know that they are Chinese. My son was very excited one day when he saw what he thought was an authentic representation of a Chinese man in an old Charlie Chan movie.

The dilemma for a second-generation Chinese-American who is a parent is very difficult. If he is not working or living in the Chinese community, he finds not only that his orientation and attitudes are completely American, but that his ability to speak Chinese has become rusty. The second-generation Chinese-American, although he has not faced real racial prejudice as the Negroes have or even as the Japanese in America have, nevertheless has been subjected to curiosity. He is, in a word, tired of being quaint and patronized. He is tired of the constant barrage of questions from well-intentioned people about Chinese culture, politics and tong wars. The reaction, then, is to turn his back on it all and rub it out. This, he soon finds, is hopeless because he looks Chinese.

Almost every Chinese-American at some point during his life goes through a period of finding his identity. Is he Chinese or American? Unfortunately, most of them find it difficult, if not impossible, to be both in this country of hyphenated Americans. We are therefore faced, in spite of the great efforts of the elders to build new Chinese schools, with the extinction of a great cultural heritage.

CHAPTER 6

Chinese Beliefs

The religious beliefs of the "heathen Chinese" have fascinated Americans for over a century. No guided tour to Chinatown is complete without a visit to a "joss house" or Chinese temple. As early as 1850 three hundred "China Boys," as they were called in those days, were invited to what turned out to be a prayer meeting in San Francisco. Organized by Vice-Consul Frederick A. Woodworth, Reverend Albert Williams, a Mr. Buel and others, the white fathers ordered copies of the Scriptures in Chinese from Canton to distribute at this meeting. A newspaper account which appeared in the *Daily Alta California,* on August 26, 1850, described it this way:

> . . . The dissemination of Scriptural truths among the members of a nation otherwise highly civilized, is a great and good object; and when we consider the remarkable intelligence of the Chinese, their aptitude and capacity for acquiring knowledge, we cannot do less than believe that the happiest results will follow this praiseworthy attempt to diffuse among them Christian doctrines and useful knowledge.

The meeting took place at Portsmouth Square in San Francisco and it was reported that the "China Boys" appeared dressed in their "holiday attire" with their pigtails neatly braided. They were welcomed by Mayor Geary, and after a few short speeches translated into Chinese by an interpreter, Reverend T. D. Hunt tried to describe a Celestial Heaven where the "China Boys" could live forever and never die if they were good on earth. His message was met by laughter from the audience.

A few years later Dr. William Speer, formerly a Presbyterian missionary in China, opened the first Chinese mission in the United States and started the home mission movement. In 1859, after ill health had forced Dr. Speer to abandon his work, Reverend A. W. Loomis, also a man with experience as a missionary in China, resumed the work. He opened the first "public" evening school for Chinese for the study of English and attempted to continue the health clinic in the mission which Dr. Speer started. Both Dr. Speer and Reverend Loomis became good friends of the Chinese and were practically their sole defenders when the waves of prejudice appeared. Their work sparked the whole home mission movement so that today there is at least one such mission in each of the Chinatowns. But the number of conversions among the laboring immigrants has always been very small.

The first immigrants to California and Nevada built joss houses for their sacred figures, candles, and incense urns in the form of log cabins. It is not clear whether the word "joss" came from "josh" or from the Portuguese word "deos" meaning god. Most of these temples had as their principal holy image a figure of Kwan Kung, the military hero of the Three Kingdoms, also known as the god of war. There were no meetings or services. The temples were used only in periods of need or for offerings at certain times of the year.

These ritualistic practices have puzzled Westerners who have tried, usually in vain, to discover from them the religious beliefs of the non-intellectual contemporary Chinese. Actually, the typical unschooled Cantonese immigrant is a religious and ethical eclectic, drawing the kernels of his beliefs from Confucianism, Buddhism, and Taoism, the three great religions of China. But in the process of oral transmission through many generations, and the confusion which so often accompanies eclecticism, the purity of the original doctrines has become clouded. Though there was no polytheism in original Confucianism or Taoism, and nothing that a Westerner would call theology in original Buddhism, the uneducated contemporary Chinese is polytheistic and accepts, if he ever thinks about such things at all, certain bits of superstition, mysticism, and aspects of ancestor worship that are distortions of doctrines from the three great religious philosophies that are his heritage. The average man is unable to identify himself as a Confucianist, a Buddhist, or a Taoist.

This is not surprising in a people who have always respected the religious beliefs of others and have found no inconsistency in accepting parts of the beliefs of several religions. It is a phenomenon which is typical of the Far East. No one in China would find any incongruity in the same family using the ritual from one religion for a marriage ceremony, that of another for celebrating a birth, and that of a third for marking a funeral. Long before St. Paul said "Prove all things, hold fast that which is good," Eastern philosophy advocated it and Orientals practiced it.

What is to be regretted is not the eclecticism, but the distortions of the original doctrines of all three of the great religions and the additions of concepts entirely foreign to the philosophies of their founders.

Of the three religions of China, two of them, Confucianism and Taoism, were originally modifications of a much older religion, some record of which is found in the ancient Chinese Classics which Confucius and his disciples edited. The third, Buddhism, is an importation from India. All three have been corrupted in the eclecticism which makes up the corpus of beliefs of the contemporary uneducated Chinese.

As early as the Shang period, (1766–1123 B.C.) there were references to a deity called Shang-ti, a divine ruler who watched over human society and controlled the working of the universe. A number of lesser deities reigned under him. God of the Old Testament is referred to in translations as Shang-ti.

It was believed by the ancient Chinese that their departed ancestors lived with Shang-ti in a vague undefined region and could influence the fortunes of the living. Sacrifices and offerings of food were made to these ancestors and incense and candles burned in their honor particularly in times of need, such as drought, fire, or famine. During the Chou period, (1122–255 B.C.) only kings made sacrifices to Shang-ti while the common people had to use their ancestors as intermediaries. Offerings were also made during New Year's and Ch'ing Ming—an annual period for paying respects to the dead. The Chinese in America still observe Ch'ing Ming, though this is no longer a worship but a custom and tradition indicating filial piety and respect for elders.

This attitude toward elders is a part of the ancient tradition of China. It is, of course, the subject of the *Book of Filial Piety*, one of the classics edited by Confucius. On a visit to Chinatown, you may find among the figures for sale a ceramic group which will puzzle you until you know what it represents. Before a young woman a very old and feeble man is half-kneeling, leaning, leaning on his staff, and is suckling at one of the very full breasts of the woman. This is an illustration of one of the classic stories in the *Book of Filial Piety*, in which a young woman who has recently borne a child thus nourishes her toothless father who is unable to eat solid food.

As well as Shang-ti there is in the ancient Chinese concept, Tien, translated as "heaven," but not meaning a place like the Christian paradise, in which the righteous

souls find eternal life after death. Rather the term connotes a universal ruling order, corresponding, perhaps, to
the Brahman in Hinduism, and the Logos in Greek
philosophy ("the Word" in the Gospel according to
John).

The creative force of the universe was embodied in the
two opposing, yet complementary forces, each powerless
without the other. The Yang is the male, the positive, the
bright, the warm, the effusive. It connotes sun, fire, heat,
heaven, dominance, spring, and summer among other
things. The Yin is the female, the negative, the dark, the
secretive and silent, the deep, the earthly. It connotes
the moon, cold, water, earth, recessiveness, autumn, and
winter. The symbol of the two is a perfect circle tightly
containing two interlocked embryonic figures, one white
and one black, looking a bit like two tadpoles. Offspring
of the Yang were a host of good spirits called *shen;* from
the Yin came evil spirits called *kwei.* These inhabited
man and accounted for the duality of his nature. They
also inhabited every bush and tree, and lay in wait at
every turn of the road. Carrying lighted torches at night,
and beating on gongs, drums, and kettles, would often
frighten them away, and the heavenly *shen,* which included both gods and departed ancestors, and which
were more powerful than the *kwei,* would protect the
righteous on earth who offered sacrifices and prayers.

Confucius did not organize a new cult, nor did he attempt to reform an old one in the sense in which Jesus
attempted to reform the Judaism of his time, and
Gautama the Hinduism to which he was born. Rather
Master Kung (which is a literal translation of his Chinese name) attempted to systematize one which had existed in the land of his birth from time immemorial. The
emphasis of his teachings was on the proprieties and
moral behavior, rather than on theology or worship. He
is reported to have used the term Shang-ti only once,

and when asked about it to have replied, "I prefer not speaking." He preferred the less personal Tien, and spoke often of "the ordinances of Heaven." "The superior man," he said, "stands in awe of the ordinances of Heaven." He was not concerned, he said, because men did not know him, for Heaven knew him. When asked what constituted wisdom, he answered, "To give one's self earnestly to the duties due to men, and, while respecting spiritual beings, to keep aloof from them, may be called wisdom." He stated the Golden Rule in the negative form used by Rabbi Hillel half a millennium later, "What you do not want done to yourself, do not do to others."

He believed in a moral order in the universe, but his belief did not involve the invocation of divinity. Nor did he discuss life after death as a deterrent to wickedness or as a stimulant to virtue. When asked about it he answered, "While you cannot know about life, how can you know about death?"

There has been much discussion as to whether Confucianism, even in its original form as promulgated by the great Master Kung is, or is not, a religion. I do not wish to join the argument here on either side. The answer to the question for any individual depends upon his definition of the word "religion." The imperishable moral precepts which Confucius left behind him are essentially those of all the great religions, though there are differences in emphasis, just as there are between the doctrines of different sects in the same basic religion. What matters is that the Confucian precepts concerning filial piety, righteousness, benevolence, and the proprieties teach men how to live and what to live for.

Side by side with Confucianism there developed in China the second of her great religious philosophies, Taoism, both products of the sixth century B.C. While Confucius, the realist, spoke chiefly of human behavior and the understandable events of the physical world,

Lao Tze, the mystic, spoke chiefly of the unseen and intangible, often emphasizing philosophic truths by paradox. His philosophy emphasized the concept of the Yang and the Yin, and found in "the Tao" "a thing inherent and natural which existed before heaven and earth . . . it may be regarded as the mother of the universe."

What is "Tao"? The answer is very difficult, for the meaning cannot be pinned down to a single precise definition. It has often been translated as "the Way," or "the Path." It has also been rendered as "reason," "nature," "God," and as "the Word," in the sense of the Greek *Logos*. The first verse of the Gospel according to John in Chinese translations reads, "In the beginning was the Tao, and the Tao was with God, and the Tao was God . . ." Obviously there is no single English word which can adequately express the concept of Tao. As a matter of fact, the author of the *Tao Te King*, supposedly Lao Tze, seems to have intimated the hopelessness of definition, for instead of attempting to define it he lists its qualities and some of its affects on the natural world. It "seems to be the origin of all things." It "looks like the predecessor of nature." It is "the mystic mother." It "seems ever to endure. In use it can never be exhausted." It stabilizes everything, for, "where Tao is equilibrium is. When Tao is lost, out comes all the differences in things." It is "invisible and intangible, yet there are forms . . . substance . . . essence in it." It is "supreme." "By it all things come into being and it does not reject them." Yet "it does not claim mastery over them." It "is ever inactive, yet there is nothing that it does not do." It is "the nameless simplicity."

Confucianism and Taoism have often been contrasted as religio-philosophic systems which were opposed to each other. Actually they complemented, rather than contradicted, each other. Where Confucianism was rigid in its demand for ceremonies and the proprieties, Taoism was permissive. To greatly oversimplify its central message one might say that it advocated letting nature take its course. Certainly it preached simplicity in all things. The man of Tao is simple "like an infant." He is humble and he thus "remains entire." He "knows where to stop." He "stays in places others despise," he "loves quietude." He "makes no fuss," etc.

These are the simple doctrines which are at the heart of the often abstruse, mystical, classical Taoism, the followers of which, according to Taoist stories, were constantly scornful of the complex conventionalities of Confucianism. But when it came to the socio-ethical doctrines of the two beliefs there is little to distinguish between them. One who lived as a good Taoist lived also as a good Confucianist, and vice versa.

Original Buddhism, that is, the doctrine of Gautama the Buddha, was, like that of Confucianism without an expressed theology. By implication Gautama denied the existence of Brahma, the central universal power of Brahmanical Hinduism, whose various powers were given the names of gods. He accepted the existence of "the gods," but believed that they were fallible beings as greatly in need of salvation as were men. As in Confucianism there was no worship, but the acceptance of "the four noble truths," concerning universal suffering caused by indulging desires, and the need to suppress such desires and to follow the "noble eightfold path" of right belief, right aspiration, right speech, right action, right livelihood, and right meditation, in order to gain Nirvana, and thus avoid rebirth and the repetition of suffering. Nirvana, like Tao, is difficult to define, and has often been erroneously called "nothingness." Gautama himself never clearly explained what he meant by the word, and after his death it was variously interpreted by different sects of Buddhism. All that can definitely be said about it is that it is a state in which rebirths need not occur again. It is also, apparently, a state of peace and blessedness.

The socio-ethical code of original Buddhism is one of the most exalted which has ever been a part of any religion. Many comparisons have been made between it and that of Judeo-Christianity, which show the large number of identical social principles in both, and the number of similar traditions in the stories of the births, ministries, and lives of Gautama and Jesus.

But before Buddhism had reached China (at about the time of the birth of Jesus) it had already gone through changes and divisions into sects. The Mahayana sect, which entered China, had deified the man who worshiped no gods, and prayed to him. Further, they looked forward to another coming of a Buddha, Maitreya, who would save the world, much as the early apostles of Christianity, and some fundamentalist Christians today, look forward to a second coming of Jesus Christ.

At about the time that Buddhism entered China, preparation for the deification of Confucius also set in. He was given the title "*Duke Ni*, all complete and illustrious." Half a century later sacrifices to his spirit were ordered by imperial edict. Toward the end of the fifth century A.D. he was canonized, and in 1906 an imperial decree named him "Co-assessor with the deities of Heaven and Earth."

Thus the two great ethical teachers, Gautama the Buddha, and Confucius, each of whom avoided theological questions in their emphasis on social righteousness, have themselves become worshiped as gods.

These are the three religions which have been the basis for the eclectic religion of the uneducated contemporary Chinese. Little is left of original Taoism or Buddhism. But the moral precepts of Confucius are taught from childhood in China and this old country practice is carried on in America with Chinese-American children, whether or not it is identified as Confucianism. In Sacramento, a large Chinese Community Center called Confucius Temple was built a few years ago housing a large meeting hall, classrooms for Chinese language schools for American-born youngsters, and a gymnasium.

A Chinese, whether he calls himself a Buddhist, a Taoist, or even a Christian never ceases to be a Confucianist. The Confucian philosophy has become an inseparable part of the society and thought of its people.

For the visitor to Chinatown particularly during the Chinese New Year, the Taoistic religious practices and influence probably have the most interesting effects. It is this religion which has introduced the symbolism of fireworks, cymbals, drums, colors, and dragons following the principle of *yang* and *yin*.

It is popularly believed that these two opposite forces succeed each other in a cycle as a law of nature. The purpose of the New Year's noisemakers is to inhibit the undesirable *yin* force or *kwei* and stimulate the operation of the *yang* force or *shen* in their influence on human beings. This religion has been called "exorcising polytheism" because of its long list of immortals and spirits connected with an abundance of magic and hocuspocus including palmistry, fortune-telling, and a trilogy for the purpose of exorcism of evil spirits representing *kwei* or *yin* forces.

To further complicate the matter, the evil spirits are divided into those which can be exorcised and those that cannot. Those that cannot are called *ching*, which are working under the auspices of Tao or nature and must therefore be borne with resignation as fate and can be eliminated only by redemption through acts of merit, self-humiliation, or sacrifices. The other spirits called the Yen are considered unauthorized by heaven and therefore can be exorcised by certain practices to bring about the *yang* cycle. According to this Taoist principle nature helps those who help themselves and he accomplishes this by the use of light and fire. Light and fire being *yang* elements are dangerous for bad spirits and are the favorite means of eliminating them.

As early as the sixth century fires were kindled on New Year's Day and bamboo thrown into them to create explosions to frighten away the bad ghosts. These pieces of bamboo were, of course, the predecessors of the firecracker.

Since loud explosive noises help to eliminate or exorcise spirits, it follows that noise of all sorts will also serve as a defense against demonry. The chief instruments of exorcising noises are gongs, cymbals, and drums. Add to these noisemakers replicas of demon-dispelling dragons, unicorns, and lions, and you have the traditional Chinese New Year's parade.

One of the most famous demon dispellers is the dragon, which is *yang*. It has the horns of a deer, the head of a camel, a demon's eyes, the neck of a snake, a tortoise's viscera, a hawk's claws, the palms of a tiger, the ears of a cow, which, however, do not hear, its horns functioning as organs of hearing. The unicorn, like the dragon, portends peace and prosperity. It has the body of a deer, a horse's hoofs, the tail of an ox, and a single horn with a fleshy growth on the tip. It feeds on no living thing.

Taoism's concentration on harmony with nature, freedom of the spirit and its emphasis on simplicity inspired Chinese art and enlightened Chinese thought. Through its symbols, ceremonies, and folklore, Chinese festivals have been enriched with the romantic, carefree, and gay carnival spirit.

Indicative of the syncretism of Buddhism, Taoism, and Confucianism, popular prints of the Three Deities show the Buddha sitting in the center flanked by Confucius and Lao Tze on either side. Some say that this is an in-

[1] A Chinese immigrant prospecting for gold in California in the year 1852. *California Historical Society, San Francisco*

[2] A page from a periodical published by J. M. Hutchings, circa 1855, depicting a Chinese battle in Weaverville, California. *California Historical Society, San Francisco*

[3] Chinese immigrants toiling at placer mining in California. *California Historical Society, San Francisco*

[4] Street scene in early Chinatown in San Francisco, circa 1882. *California Historical Society, San Francisco*

[5] Opium smokers in an underground den in San Francisco, circa 1900. *California Historical Society, San Francisco*

[6] The rubble of San Francisco's Chinatown after the earthquake and fire in 1906. *California Historical Society, San Francisco*

[7] The interior of a Chinese grocery store on Clay Street in San Francisco, 1908. *California Historical Society, San Francisco*

[8] A peddler supplies Chinese vegetables in San Francisco, early twentieth century. *Arnold Genthe Collection, California Historical Society, San Francisco*

[9] A public letter writer enscribes Chinese characters for immigrants to send home. *California Historical Society, San Francisco*

[10] Busy daytime scene in the Street of the Gamblers, San Francisco. *Arnold Genthe Collection, California Historical Society, San Francisco*

[11] An elegant mandarin is protected on promenade by a body-guard, San Francisco. *Arnold Genthe Collection, California Historical Society, San Francisco*

[12] Chinese travelers in California pause for refreshments. Note queue. *California Historical Society, San Francisco*

[13] Houses on stilts house Chinese fishermen in Monterey, California, early twentieth century. *California Historical Society, San Francisco*

dication that Buddhism became the most important religion in China, but others argue that the Buddha is sitting at his seat of importance because he is a guest. Be that as it may, Buddhism has had an enduring effect on the popular religion of China and it added not only a new way of thinking but also new gods and goddesses of Mahayana to the already crowded pantheon.

The common man in China adopted the Buddha as a demi-god and added him to the others. Taoism copied Buddhism wholesale by establishing temples, monks, scriptures, and doctrines. The Mahayana school gave a high place to the Bodhisattva, literally meaning "being of enlightment." A Bodhisattva through discipline, moral conduct, meditation or otherwise is enlightened and qualified to enter Nirvana and become a Buddha but rejects this privilege in order to remain on earth to work for the salvation of the unenlightened. Through Buddhism the common man had a religion in which everyone could be a lay Buddha although few became monks or nuns. It offered through its mythology, devotions, and compassionate and merciful Bodhisattvas a personal religion for the masses with an atmosphere of warmth which they had never experienced before.

The most popular Bodhisattva was Kwan Yin, the Goddess of Mercy, whose name means "one who hears prayer." Kwan Yin has a most interesting background. She was a male deity in India called Avalokitesvara worshiped by one school of Buddhism from A.D. 300 to 700. He was the protector of mariners and the saviour of the faithful from danger. Around the sixth century when he was transferred to China, he somehow became a female deity. Kwan Yin is the personification of gentleness, beauty, and mercy and is the ideal of Chinese womanhood. She is invoked especially by women in cases of childlessness and dangers of childbirth and she also hears the prayers of all who are in danger. She was adopted by the Taoists and occupied an important position in the popular religion of the people.

In a visit to Chinatown you will find cheap but graceful figures of her in wood or ceramic.

Compelled to compete with Buddhism and Taoism, there arose what was called "neo-Confucianism" during the Sung Dynasty, which dated from A.D. 960 to 1279. Having already absorbed some Taoist metaphysics, neo-Confucianism now sought to explain Confucian ethics metaphysically. We find the neo-Confucianists echoing the Buddhist idea that the universe is ceaselessly destroyed and re-created, but reinterpreted in Taoistic terms, as a function of the operation of the *yin* and *yang*.

Popular religion, a syncretism of the three faiths, derives its ethical tone from Confucian social and moral ideals, its abundance of superstitions, numerous gods, and the supernatural from popular Taoism and its more personalized worship and faith from Buddhism.

Because there have always been very few Chinese women in America, and since it has always been the custom for women to tend to the religious practices such as incense burning and offerings to gods and goddesses, the influence of Buddhism on the average Chinese in America is not as great as it is in China. Of the temples shown to American tourists, the only one which is actually used by the Chinese for worship is in San Francisco, although New York has recently hired a Buddhist priest for its Chinese Community Center.

CHAPTER 7

Chinese Holidays

Celebration of the Chinese New Year attracts thousands of visitors to Chinatown, U.S.A., every year to see the fireworks and the dragon, lion and unicorn dances, to hear the beating of the drums, gongs, and cymbals, to see the colorful banners and to eat the wonderful seasonal delicacies. New Year's is the one Chinese holiday which is celebrated by almost all Chinese, even those who are completely Americanized. Other Chinese holidays, celebrated in a much quieter way, by the older Chinese are: Ch'ing Ming (Festival of the Tombs), the Moon Festival, and the Dragon Boat Festival.

New Year's is the biggest day of the Chinese calendar and is regarded as such in Chinatown, where many of the Chinese customs are carried on even though many have long since forgotten their religious significance. Even the early immigrants, who hardly ever took a day off, celebrated for a week at the New Year. There are records of Chinese dragon dances and fireworks as early as the 1850s.

The color of the season is red. The Taoist influence is quite evident as the early spring Yang forces characterized by the red of early peach blossoms, overcome the Yin forces and all of the spirits which represent the winter. From the earliest times branches and images of peach wood were fixed on New Year's Day to doors and gates to welcome the spring. Today, these are replaced by sheets of red paper expressing felicity, and oranges, tangerines, and kumquats are displayed and eaten.

The climax of the New Year's celebration is the festivity on the streets, where the lions, unicorns, and dragons dance. Traditionally celebrated at noon on New Year's Day, some Chinese in America have permitted a "sneak preview" on New Year's Eve. At noon New Year's Day, groups of lion dancers representing family and clan associations start performing simultaneously in different parts of Chinatown at the front doors of their club headquarters. The instruments of each group consist of a large drum about three feet in diameter, a large metal gong, and two or three sets of large cymbals. The lion's head is intricately made of papier-mâché colorfully decorated in red, green, yellow, and orange. The "tail" of the lion (actually the body) is of silk, about ten feet long and decorated with shiny sequins. The lion dance is done by two people—one person inside the head, manipulating its eyes and jaws, and the other inside the tail. The older village clans have white whiskered lions, while the younger clubs such as the Chinese Community Club in New York, a group of Chinese-Americans, have black whiskered ones. As the lions make their appearance, the roar of the large drums, the clanging of the cymbals and gongs, and the explosion of pack after pack of firecrackers make a deafening noise. It is doubtful whether any of these people contributing to the din are thinking about exorcising the Taoist specters. They are just having a good time.

Unfortunately, the number of lion dancers are rapidly decreasing. At their best, the lion dancers are expert gymnasts and able to leap great distances like a lion and dart back and forth gracefully. Besides being strenuous, the life of a lion dancer is further complicated by the smoke and explosion of piles of firecrackers thrown at his feet. The older men, who are the experts, have retired from this vigorous exercise and have tried to teach young Chinese boys to take over.

After being in hibernation all year, the lion rouses himself at the doorway of the club. He stirs and stretches slowly until he is ready to move out of his home and perform his annual task of wishing all the people, family associations, and businesses a happy and prosperous New Year.

From the window, balcony, or fire escape of a clan association, the members dangle a head of lettuce, a tangerine, and a large red envelope called *li see*, containing money, in varying amounts. The lion slowly chews up the vegetable and fruit and pockets the money or slips it quickly to a nearby assistant with a large briefcase for that purpose. Finally the lion makes three big bows before his benefactors in acknowledgment of their gifts and moves along. Each store and restaurant also gives gifts to the performing clubs. The money goes to the treasuries of the clubs. The performers themselves get *li see* from the clubs and a banquet on New Year's Night.

The duration of the lion dance depends on the size of the Chinatown and the number of *li see* the lion has to receive from the local merchants and associations. But the New Year's celebration is not over when the lion stops dancing in the streets. Relatives and friends must be visited.

The caller usually brings a large bag of oranges and tangerines and gives *li see* to the children. The hostess offers him a cup of tea, some melon seeds—seeds symbolizing a wish for progeny—and some of her homemade New Year's pastries. As the visitor departs he leaves behind his red or pink engraved calling card. The hostess insists that he take back some of the oranges and tangerines which he brought and says: "You are too generous, please take some back." After a brief argument, the visitor properly takes a few back from the hostess.

For the family associations this is the beginning of a very busy season. Members of the clan pay their yearly dues, and plans are made for the New Year's banquet, which may take place as late as a month after New Year's Day.

For the very few Chinese in America who observe the Chinese calendar, the holiday season officially begins on the twenty-fourth day of the last month when traditionally all immortals report to the Yu Huang Ti, the "Jade Emperor" in heaven. The Jade Emperor is the chief among a great many Taoist immortals. One of these is the god of the hearth or the kitchen god, Joh-Quon, whose picture has been quietly collecting dust all year in a niche above the hearth. Suddenly he assumes new importance because he has seen and heard everything that has happened in the household throughout the year. The family fears a bad report. The solution is simple. He is bribed. The family gives him a farewell dinner of sweets so that his report will be "sweet" and after the sacrifice of food, the image of the god or the piece of paper on which the name "god of the hearth" is written is burned and he departs to heaven to make his report. On New Year's Eve a new figure of him is placed above the hearth.

Just before the New Year, Chinatowns are bustling in preparation. Housewives must decorate their homes for the holidays, cook special foods, and shop for gifts.

One blessing is that New Year's gifts are narrowly confined to traditional flowers, dwarf trees, oranges, or tangerines. Food, especially homemade food, is particularly appreciated. A popular present is the New Year's cake, a round dark brown sweet pastry, three inches thick and from eight to fifteen inches in diameter, made of rice flour, brown sugar, peanuts, and dates. Large fried balls of sweetmeats, some plain and some stuffed, are cooked to tell the future. Their shape is symbolic of the complete round of the year so, if they turn out fluffy and spherical, luck will be assured, whereas a misshapen heavy batch portends ill fortune.

In the Chinese language, the same sound often means different things and therefore the food presented may have a symbolic meaning which is signified by its name. The name for the New Year's cake is the same as the word for "high" and so the gift of the cake conveys the wish for a prosperous year. The word for duck also means "to repress" and so this offering contains a prayer that evil influences may be suppressed. The sound for chicken in certain parts of China also means "to bind" and so the bowl of chicken reflects the prayer that the family may be kept united throughout life.

The Chinese housewife is under pressure to complete preparations by midnight on New Year's Eve for, on the first day of the year, the use of a knife is prohibited, lest it should "cut luck."

In China, businessmen were also active in this last week of the year to settle all debts. If one did not do so, he would "lose face" and what is more important, his credit. This custom is not observed in the United States where Western business techniques are accepted.

While visiting at this time of year one may find the two sides of the apartment doors decorated with slips of red paper on which the occupant has written some auspicious inscription, such as "May wealth and glory become complete," "Wealth, high rank, and good salary," "May we receive the hundred blessings of Heaven," or "May Heaven send down the 5 blessings." But, because of the impersonality of apartment dwelling these luck-promising inscriptions are now found inside the apartment at the side of a makeshift altar consisting simply of an incense burner, candles and a large picture of one or more ancestors.

In the United States only a few old-fashioned families, mainly in San Francisco, observe the New Year's Eve ceremonies in which the head of the family performs the sacrifice to heaven and earth, to the household gods including the kitchen god, Joh-Quon, and to all the gods who have blessed the family during the year, and to the ancestral tablets. In this ceremony, the master of the household bows three times in front of the latter and thanks the gods for all they have done for the family and the house during the past year. The prayer ends with the burning of idol paper money (that is, pieces of rice paper on which are drawn representations of money), and a large sheet of paper bearing the images of several dozen gods. On the following day the ceremony is repeated as a prayer for the coming year.

A great deal of superstitious lore of lucky and unlucky times has grown up around twelve beasts which are used to designate calendar years. Combined with five agents, they indicate sixty-year cycles. The beasts are the rat, ox, tiger, hare, dragon, snake, horse, sheep, monkey, cock, dog, and boar. The five agents are wood, fire, earth, metal, and water. Like the *yang* and *yin*, the agents are not physical substances but metaphysical forces or modes which dominate or control certain periods of time, commonly the seasons, in fixed succession. It is accepted that they proceed in the order in which they are believed to have produced each other: wood-producing fire, fire-producing earth, earth-producing metal, metal-producing water, and so on.

When the five agents are combined with the twelve beasts to designate the sixty-year cycle we thus start with the year of the wood rat, the year of the wood ox, the wood tiger, etc. The next twelve-year cycle is affected by the second agent, fire, and again the years are designated by the twelve animals.

The use of the twelve beasts was essentially rationalistic, an ancient method of conveniently measuring time. In the Han Dynasty, cyclical signs for designating years, days, and hours were apparently in use and a set of twelve signs called the "twelve earthly branches" were used to designate the months. Another set of ten signs called the "ten heavenly stems" designated the ancient ten-day week. Sometime during the Chou Dynasty these two sets of signs were combined to form sixty binomial terms used to designate a cycle of sixty days and also a cycle of sixty years. Finally the twelve branches were used to designate twelve two-hour periods making up the day.

One festival which the visitor to Chinatown will not be able to participate in is Ch'ing Ming, the spring festival, or as it is sometimes called, the sweeping of the tombs. Ch'ing Ming, meaning pure and clear, is the only Chinese festival that is based directly and entirely on the sun and not on the moon. It falls on the 106th day after the winter solstice (December 21). The struggle between the *yang*, the power of light, and *yin*, the power of darkness, has ended in the victory of the *yang* force. Spring has finally come.

Popularized Buddhism, which removed the fear of death, influenced this festival. This is the time for commemorating the dead. Families go to the cemeteries to "sweep the tombs," to pull the weeds and perhaps to plant a tree. Red candles and idol paper money are burned next to the tombstones. Firecrackers are exploded to frighten away the specters or to help the *yang* forces against the *yin*. A little wine is poured on the tombstone. A feast for the dead and for the guardian of the spirit of the tomb is spread next to the tombstone. When the dead have partaken, the living who wait near the tomb consume the food.

In America, many of the family associations hire buses to take the whole clan out to the cemetery. Graves of persons who have no relatives in this country are taken care of by the family clansmen. Before the Communists took over China, the remains were exhumed after a few years and transferred to China, where they were reburied so that their spirits might return to their homeland. These associations or a consolidated association often would buy burial plots for the use of the Chinese because at one time many cemeteries refused to bury them.

The Dragon Boat Festival which falls on the fifth day of the fifth month of the Chinese calendar and is therefore sometimes called the "Double Fifth" was one of the most picturesque festivals in China. Again, this seasonal festival, like other seasonal celebrations, has as its purpose the harmonizing of the *yang* and the *yin*. The *yang* symbolizing the summer, reaches the peak of its power just before the summer solstice, and the *yin* comes into being and waxes until the winter solstice.

As the name of the holiday implies, it is a day of boat races, with boats shaped like dragons, the high prow showing the beast's fierce mouth and its dangerous fangs. The sides of the boats are brightly painted particularly with red, the symbol of heat, summer, and fire. On the boat are the rowers and men playing cymbals or beating gongs. Different guilds or clubs compete on this annual festival. The Dragon Boat Festival is fondly remembered by all the Chinese immigrants from the coastal provinces of Central and South China. In the evening, after boat races, the river is beautifully speckled with lantern-decorated boats parading slowly down the river. Most of the inhabitants of Chinatown have not seen a Dragon Boat race for many years but annually their memories are rekindled by the eating of *jung*, three-cornered rice dumplings consisting of glutinous rice filled with beans, pork, lotus seeds, and the yolk of a salted egg. Each portion is wrapped with five pointed bamboo leaves, resembling the demon-dispelling sword and is then boiled for about four hours. *Jung* is sold in teahouses of the larger Chinatowns.

A folk story about *jung* tells that Ch'u Yuan, a famous court poet who was also a minister and counselor to the king of Ch'u was deeply concerned with the fate of his country. Once Ch'u Yuan was greatly distressed when the king refused his advice. He departed and wandered about unhappily until he reached the river where he composed one of his most beautiful poems and then threw himself into the water and drowned. People in his country who loved and respected him threw rice into the water as a sacrifice to the dead. The soul of Ch'u Yuan appeared to a group of fishermen telling them that in spite of their sacrifices he was still starving because a huge dragon had taken away the rice they had offered. They were asked to wrap the rice in small pieces of silk and bind the packages with silk threads of five different colors. The rice dumplings, *jung,* are still eaten today in celebration of this festival, although they are now wrapped in bamboo leaves and not silk.

The Moon Festival is celebrated on the fifteenth day of the eighth month corresponding roughly to the end of September. According to the lunar calendar the fifteenth day of the month is always the day of the full moon. The moon, a *yin* symbol, represents the female element, water, darkness, and night. This festival, therefore, is a woman's festival and is celebrated at night. Sometimes called the Harvest Festival or the Moon's birthday, this is probably the most romantic of Chinese festivals although the celebration is strictly private.

Living on the moon, according to Chinese folklore, are a hare, a toad, and the old man of the moon. The hare sits under a cassia tree and pounds the elixir of life in a large mortar. Every month the large dark toad devours the moon and a few days later the moon is born again out of its mouth.

Moon cakes, *yuet beang,* large round cakes made of flour and brown sugar and decorated with likenesses of

the moon and its palaces are the special dish of this festival. When night has fallen and the moonlight from the
harvest moon has filled the courtyard, the family gathers
before an outdoor altar. On the altar is a dish of thirteen
moon cakes, thirteen being the number of months in a
complete Chinese moon year, the intercalary year of 384
days. Also on the altar are melons, pomegranates, grapes,
apples, and peaches. Melons and pomegranates having
many seeds, suggest fecundity. Apples and grapes sym-
bolize fertility, and peaches, longevity.

The woman of the house bows before the altar in honor
of the moon. Following the ceremony the women take
this opportunity of the moon's birthday to consult about
their matrimonial fate because, according to ancient Chinese tradition, marriage matches are made by Yueh Lao-
yeh, the old man of the moon.

Although very few people today actually celebrate the
Moon Festival, bakeries in Chinatown prepare moon
cakes at this time of the year and they are very popular
for snacks.

CHAPTER 8

Chinese Food

Some people, even some who visit Chinatown, never get beyond chop suey and chow mein in what they think are adventures in Chinese food. Neither of these dishes is served in China; both are Chinese-styled American food. Chop suey, in Chinese, means to chop finely, i.e., to hash. There is an interesting story, which may or may not be true, explaining the origin of the dish. In the 1860s, very late one night, some hungry California miners went looking for food. The only place still open was a tiny Chinese restaurant which had never served Occidentals before. The little Chinese man who doubled as waiter and cook was ready to close up but being unable to communicate with his strange customers and furthermore being much smaller than the large, powerful-looking, hungry miners, he threw together what was left over and served it. The men loved it and asked what the dish was called. The rest is history. There is hardly a town or city with over a population of 25,000 that does not have a Chinese restaurant. And, more often than not, the words CHOP SUEY or CHOW MEIN are advertised prominently in front of it.

At the turn of the century, many state laws prohibited Chinese from engaging in some occupations. One which avoided open competition with labor unions and Caucasians was the restaurant business and thus the Oriental immigrant was permitted to enter it. The growth in the number of Chinese restaurants was phenomenal and by the 1920s, about the time of the mah jong craze, one of the early peaks in Chinese cooking was reached. The Roaring Twenties and the age of prohibition brought with it dozens of huge, magnificent Chinese restaurants with dance floors and entertainment. Few of them were able to survive after prohibition when the night club business flourished again.

At first, only chop suey and chow mein were popular, but as Americans became interested in Chinese cooking they began to try other dishes. Soon the Chinese menu was greatly expanded to include lobster Cantonese, egg rolls, sweet and sour pork, roast duck, spare ribs, and many other dishes. For the adventurous, it is not difficult to find restaurants that serve bird's nest soup and shark's fin soup.

As more and more people wanted to eat in the "real" Chinese way, restaurants innovated the so-called "family dinners," which included soup, egg rolls and a number of dishes to be selected, depending on how many people were eating.

In a Chinese restaurant you should order one dish for each person present, although no hard and fast rule can be made because of the varying size of the dishes. For four people you might, for example, order a soup, a seafood dish, a chicken dish, a pork dish, and perhaps an egg dish or beef with vegetables. The purpose is variety not only in taste but also in texture.

The way in which the ingredients of a dish are cut, i.e., diced, sliced, or minced, can affect its taste because of the difference in texture. If a dice-cut dish such as *char shu ding* (dice-cut roast pork with vegetables) is ordered, then you would not have *gai ding* (dice-cut chicken with vegetables) because of its similarity in texture. You might, instead, order a chicken dish such as *moo goo gai peen* (sliced chicken with mushrooms and vegetables), which will look different and have a different texture. If you order a sharp-tasting dish such as sweet and sour spare ribs, be sure to order something bland, such as vegetables, to go with it.

Chinese menus needn't puzzle you. With a glossary of a dozen or so words you can read a Cantonese menu. The names of the dishes will include the main ingredients: chicken (*gai*), duck (*opp*), beef (*ngow yok*), pork (*gee yok*), lobster (*lung har*), shrimp (*har*), fish (*yu*), noodles (*mein*), rice (*fon*), spare ribs (*pai guot*), Chinese vegetables (*bok choy*), roast pork (*char shew*), egg (*don*), soup (*tong*).

The six basic methods of Chinese cooking are also likely to appear in the names of dishes: stir-frying (*chow*), roasting (*shew*), deep frying (*jow*), steaming (*jing*), fricasseeing (*mun*), and red-roasting or cooking in soy sauce (*hoong shew*).

Put elements of this simple glossary together and you can recognize some of the dishes on a menu. Chinese deep-fried chicken is *jow gai*, barbecued spare ribs is *shew pai quot*, fried shrimp is *jow har*, steamed chicken is *jing gai*.

Words for methods of preparation also appear in the names of dishes: slicing (*peen*), dicing (*ding*), chopping or mincing (*soong*), cutting in chunks (*kow*), and shredding (*sze*). Thus you may have *chow gai kow* (stir-fried chicken cut in chunks), *gai ding* (diced chicken with vegetables), *ngow yok soong* (minced beef).

China has hundreds of schools of cooking which can be broken down basically into those of Canton, Fukien, Honan, Shantung, and Szechuan provinces.

Canton is the southernmost province of China and because of its rich soil and favorable climate there is an abundance of raw materials, a variety of vegetables, meats and seafoods. This school of cooking has the largest repertoire of dishes. It is the best known both abroad and in China. It has the most international appeal as it does not depend on any particular or unusual seasonings. Its quick stir-fry dishes (using little oil), make up 90 percent of the menus in most Chinese restaurants in America.

Cantonese banquets and steamed delicacies are especially well known. The use of squab and turtle originated in Canton.

Fukien is a seacoastal province adjacent to Canton which produces the finest soy sauce in China. The Fukien school of cooking is famous for its preparation of seafood and its emphasis on soups. The Fukienese are so fond of soups that one quarter of their meals may consist of them.

The Honan school of cooking has richer dishes than that of Fukien. The few dishes that the cooks of Honan prepare are excellent. They are especially fond of spicy, hot, and sweet and sour dishes. Sweet and sour spare ribs probably originated in Honan. Their most famous dish is bear's paw, an ancient delicacy in China. Bear's paws are mentioned in the works of Mencius, (371?-288? B.C.) the great commentator on Confucian doctrine. Mencius said, "I like fish and I also like bear's paws. If I cannot have the two together, I will let the fish go, and take the bear's paws. So, I like life, and I also like righteousness. If I cannot keep the two together, I will let life go and choose righteousness."

The Shantung school of the north has surprisingly few *chow* or stir-fry dishes. The food tends to be lighter and prepared in wine stock or soft fried. Although not many of its dishes are famous, its truly superb Peking duck is any gourmet's delight.

Szechuan is a middle western province with food which tends to be hot, seasoned with garlic, and oily. This area also has rich soil and favorable climate but has not taken full advantage of this in its cooking.

Among true gourmets (Chinese or otherwise) there is general agreement that the Cantonese school of cooking is far superior in variety as well as splendor. Until after World War II, almost all Chinese restaurants in this country were Cantonese.

The great majority of early Chinese immigrants in

America were Cantonese. After World War II a great number of Chinese refugees from other provinces were stranded here, many of them finding it difficult to find work. Hitherto the non-Cantonese, mainly from Shanghai, were very careful to differentiate themselves from the Cantonese because the image of the Chinese in America was that of the laundryman or restaurantman, and these better educated and more affluent persons did not want to be grouped with that class. However, with the problems of racial discrimination in industry and difficulty of communication, a number of these non-Cantonese started opening restaurants. These restaurants can now be found in the larger cities claiming to serve what they call "true Chinese cuisine" and differentiating themselves from the Cantonese restaurants by generally calling themselves Northern or Mandarin restaurants.

As a matter of pure geography the term "northern" is a misnomer, as these restaurants serve Fukien as well as Szechuan dishes. Szechuan is a western province. Canton is the southernmost province of China but by no means comprises all of South China. Fukien is also southern. Fukien is to Canton what Georgia is to Florida. Some people would have you believe that the Mason-Dixon Line of China is drawn at the borders of Canton.

Sauntering through Chinatown one will find different kinds of eating places. The most familiar are the large nicely decorated places which cater mainly to the American trade. In these restaurants one will find the family dinners and a rather complete menu. They are wonderful places to dine out, offering complete multi-course dinners. Some of them serve cocktails.

During lunchtime in New York, San Francisco, and Los Angeles the Chinese merchant usually lunches at a teahouse enjoying *dim sum* (which literally means "dot the heart"). The meal is sometimes called tiffin or high tea in the British manner. There is *har gow*, shrimp dumpling in

which shrimp and other ingredients are wrapped with
delicate rice flour dough that becomes translucent when
steamed. This same dough is used to make a half-moon
shaped dumpling filled with chopped meat called *fun
quor*. *Sui mei* is chopped pork with finely diced bamboo
shoots and water chestnuts, wrapped in a yellow dough
called *wonton* skin. Other varieties of *sui mei* are made
with the same meat filler stuffed onto the top of a large
black Chinese mushroom. Sometimes the filler is put on
top of a piece of wintermelon, or fancily arranged on top
of a whole shrimp.

Wonderful little buns called *bow,* that look like delicately puffed snowballs, are the Chinese form of sand-
wiches. Various types of fillers are used inside of the *bow.*
Char shu bow is filled with roast pork and a delicious
barbecue sauce; *jeel yeen bow* is filled with peanut butter
and sesame seed; *year see bow* is filled with coconut
shreds and brown sugar; *dow sar bow* is filled with black
sugar. Sometimes there is *gai bow,* filled with chopped
chicken and Chinese mushrooms, bamboo shoots, and water chestnuts; and occasionally there is a house special
called *dai bow,* extra large and filled with the chef's favorite ingredients.

Fun guen looks like a steamed white egg roll. The outside is made from rice flour, and the inside is filled with
shredded roast pork, bamboo shoots, and other vegetables. There are a few deep fried *dim sum* dishes, such
as *woo gok.* This is half-moon shaped, uses taro as the
covering and is filled with pork. This dish is seasonal since
taro is not available all year round. *Lor bok go* is made
from Chinese turnips mixed with Chinese sausage and
dried shrimps and is pan fried.

For anyone seeking to find out about Chinese food, having *dim sum* is a must. *Dim sum* is generally served only
during lunch. It is entirely different from anything that is
served at dinners and is an experience not to be missed.

So different is the way of preparation of this food that the restaurants which serve them must have a separate cooking staff. The following restaurants serve it daily: in New York, Pagoda Restaurant, Lee's, Nom Wah, Bo Bo; in San Francisco, Yank Sing, Hang Ah Tea Room, and Songhay Tea House; in Los Angeles, New Moon Café and Man Fook Low. In Washington, D.C., the Nanking. In Chicago, Philadelphia, and Boston *dim sum* is served only on Sundays.

The Chinese are very fond of *seel year*, midnight snacks, and for this reason you may find tiny restaurants, many of them in basements, open practically all night. They are called noodle shops or *jook* shops. *Jook*, called congee in English, is a thick soup made by cooking a little rice with lots of water for a number of hours. To plain *jook* is added fish filet, beef, dried scallops or dried squid depending on what you want. Chinese teenagers, who are Chinese only in physical appearance and eating habits, jam these little noodle shops and *jook* shops on Saturday nights after big dances. There generally is no American menu for these places because their clientele is mostly Chinese. The specials of the day are written on strips of red paper and pasted on the walls around the room. Noodle shops are fun not only for midnight snacks but for any time of the day.

The Chinese are very fond of noodles for lunches and snacks. In some provinces noodles are eaten instead of rice as a staple. It is believed that Marco Polo brought the noodle to Italy from China. Generally it is *don mein*, egg noodle, which is served. Unlike the short deep fried noodles served in commercial chow mein, the *don mein* are soft, like spaghetti. There is *lo mein*, with roast pork, beef or shrimp. The noodles are stir-fried with a little oil, soy sauce, *bok choy* (a leafy green vegetable) and either roast pork, beef or shrimp. In Cantonese chow mein, the noodles are first pan fried so they are slightly toasted, then topped with shredded roast pork and vegetables. *Wuey mein* is a slightly wider noodle (without egg). Noodles are also served in soup much like the American chicken noodle soup except that there are more noodles, the noodles come in long strands and each bowl is generally enough for a whole meal in itself. A much grander noodle soup dish is *yang chow wor mein*. Served in a large soup vat, the soup and noodles are topped with large pieces of roast duck, chicken, black Chinese mushrooms, roast pork, chicken livers and gizzards, shrimps, bamboo shoots, Chinese cabbage, and other ingredients. Another kind of noodle is called *fun*. White and about one-inch wide, it has a very smooth texture. It too can be served either in soup or stir-fried.

A somewhat different sort of eating place in Chinatown is the "rice house," *fon deem*, which advertises itself as economical. Besides a few little tables, many of these little places use lunch counters to serve their customers, who are generally bachelors and working men. Economical they are. For less than a dollar the customer can order a plate full of rice topped with his favorite ingredients. *Fon care ngow yok fon* is rice topped with tomatoes and beef and gravy. Pork chop *fon* is a fried pork chop on top of rice, *hambork fon* is a hamburger (fried in soy sauce) on top of rice; and *gar lay ngow yok fon* is curried beef with rice.

These little rice houses also specialize in real home-cooked dishes. Many of the dishes served in the fancier restaurants would not be served in the average Chinese home every day but only for company or special occasions. The little rice houses serve humble everyday fare such as salted fish, salted cabbage, steamed beef with salted dried cabbage, steamed fish, steamed pork with ham, and salted eggs.

Since the Chinese are generally known as tea drinkers, it is somewhat surprising to find a great number of coffee shops in Chinatown. This is one American habit which the Chinese in America have acquired. A few varieties of *dim sum* are served with coffee, as well as custard tarts, baked buns, steamed sponge cake, and almond cookies. These coffee shops are frequented in the morning by chefs, waiters, and other restaurant people for a quick breakfast on the way to work. In recent years the coffee shops have became stiff competition for the teahouses. Because of their speed and informality, they are preferred to the teahouses by persons who are eating by themselves. For the visitor to Chinatown, whose feet are weary from walking, the coffee shops are the best places for a pause and small snack.

In the windows of Chinese grocery stores will be displayed fresh Chinese vegetables brought in every day by truck farmers. *Bok choy*, Chinese celery cabbage, with large bright green leaves and white stalks, looks like a cross between celery and cabbage and is the most popularly used vegetable both in Chinese homes and restaurants. It is the vegetable filler for practically every dish in a Chinese menu and you will find it diced and sliced, and the leaves used in soups. A shorter and squatter vegetable with green stalks is *guy choy*. It has a slightly bitter flavor and is often used in soups. Chinese parsley is different from American parsley, having a strong scent of flowers. It is used as a garnish. Melons and squashes of various sizes and shapes will catch your eye. The most prominent of these is wintermelon. It is the size of a large pumpkin with a whitish green exterior. The inside is pulpy and white. Customers usually buy only a section or two of this to make soup although sometimes the gourmet will buy the whole melon and make the soup right inside of the melon for a wonderful dish called *dung quar jhung*. *Jeet quar*, which looks like a squash in size and shape, has an unusual green fuzzy skin, and for that reason it is often called hairy melon.

Also in the window you will find delicate snow pea pods which look like ordinary small flat pea pods but which are delicately sweet when cooked. These snow peas are difficult to grow and consequently often cost more per pound than a good steak.

Walking into the Chinese grocery store you cannot help smelling a number of different odors. At first you may notice the odor of the dried salted fish. Heavily salted, only a small piece of this fish is steamed with a meal. Nearby may be large opened tins of preserved ducks soaking in oil, and also *dow foo,* or bean curd, consisting of white squares made from soy bean and called the poor man's meat because it is high in protein.

Across the room your eye may be attracted to large brown barrels of *shuen choy,* pickled cabbage, or perhaps salted ducks' eggs. Baskets filled with *ngar choy,* bean sprouts, are displayed. Near the meat counter are bunches of *lop chang,* Chinese sausages hanging each on a string.

Finally you will notice the shelves all around the room containing many of the condiments needed to prepare a Chinese dinner. There are soy sauces in bottles and cans, oyster sauce, cans of bamboo shoots, water chestnuts, and packages of *dung goo,* Chinese mushrooms. There will be jars and cans of *shuen moy jeung* (commonly called duck sauce in Chinese restaurants) into which spare ribs, roast duck and egg rolls are dipped. Deep crimson haisein sauce is used in the preparation of spare ribs. Brown bean sauce, *mien see,* which comes in square cans, is used for the preparation of steamed fish. You will find boxes of bird's nest, looking like brownish snowflakes, and also boxes of *fun see,* "cellophane noodles" (rice noodles so named because they become transparent when cooked) used for garnish and also cooked with meats. Many types of teas will be displayed. The most popular is Oolong, a black tea. Jasmine tea is the favorite flower tea.

If you ask the clerk, he will bring you fresh *don mein*, egg noodles, or egg roll wrappers or wonton skin from the refrigerator. Perhaps you may want to take home a box of almond cookies or fortune cookies made locally in Chinatown for the children.

CHAPTER 9

A Visit to Chinatown

The word Chinatown still evokes in many people's minds the image of tong wars (though the last one occurred in the 1930s), opium dens, and sinister crimes. Even today, guides can make tourists believe wild and fantastic descriptions of the "goings on" in Chinatown. The Chinese businessman tolerates this so long as it is good for business.

The enjoyment of Chinatown cannot be gotten from a quick guided tour. The pleasures and insights of a leisurely all-day excursion through its streets and alleyways are your rewards if you have listened to the exotic sounding voices, tasted the wondrous food, touched a cool smooth piece of jade, or a bolt of fine embroidered silk, and gotten to know the people.

In the early days, one perhaps identified Chinatown more by its smell than by its appearance. With the exception of that in Los Angeles, the architecture is not planned as a unit. As the Chinese colonies grew larger, restaurants catering to the inhabitants decorated their balconies with colorful silk lanterns. Shops advertised their wares with Chinese calligraphy written on store windows or carved into large wooden signs. Headquarters for family associations and clubhouses were decorated with traditional yellows and reds. It was probably not until the overthrow of the Manchu Dynasty in 1911 that the Chinese in America started to create architecturally an image of China.

Modern brick or concrete buildings decorated with

[14] Laborers drying squid at the Chinese Fishery, Monterey, early twentieth century. *California Historical Society, San Francisco*

[15] Elaborate Chinese float at the Fiesta of Los Angeles, early twentieth century. *California Historical Society, San Francisco*

[16] Grant Avenue street scene in contemporary Chinatown, San Francisco. *Phil Palmer from Monkmeyer Press Photo Service*

[17] Modern Chinese Americans strolling on Grant Avenue in San Francisco. *Phil Palmer from Free Lance Photographers Guild Inc.*

[18] Traditional architectural style in the Chinatown Telephone Exchange, San Francisco. *Phil Palmer from Free Lance Photographers Guild Inc.*

[19] Chinese and American delicacies mingle in modern Chinese grocery store, San Francisco. *Phil Palmer from Free Lance Photographers Guild Inc.*

[20] Chinese-American children studying art in present-day San Francisco. *Phil Palmer from Monkmeyer Press Photo Service*

[21] Character study of a street type in Chinatown, Chicago, Illinois, in 1891. *Courtesy Chicago Historical Society*

[22] Westworth Avenue is the heart of modern Chinatown in Chicago. *Chicago Historical Society photograph by J. Sherwin Murphy*

[23] The On Leong Tong Building (Chinese Merchants Association) is Chinatown City Hall, Chicago. *Chicago Historical Society photograph by Otho B. Turbyfill*

[24] Chinese New Year in Philadelphia is celebrated with a glamorous parade. *Jane Latta Photography*

[25] Mott Street in New York's Chinatown during a Chinese New Year Parade. *Robert Campbell from Monkmeyer Press Photo Service*

[26] Chinese Americans in New York's Chinatown in front of their church. *Merrim from Monkmeyer Press Photo Service*

[27] Traditional Chinese dragon marching in Chinese New Year parade in New York. *Robert Campbell from Monkmeyer Press Photo Service*

Chinese friezes and pillar decorations topped always with the traditional curved roofs with glazed tiles have become popular in Chinatowns all over the United States and have become known as examples of Chinese architecture. Even relatively small Chinese communities such as in Houston and Sacramento have built such buildings and Phoenix hopes to do so soon.

To the visitor, such buildings with pagoda tops or eaves add to the atmosphere of "old country" charm and lend authenticity to "little China." In most Chinatowns, there are not many such buildings. Most of the structures are tenements or stores built in conventional Western style.

It is interesting to note that architecture as such was never a profession in China. The builders were masons and carpenters. In the 1920s American-trained Chinese architects returned to China and attempted to create a new national style of architecture. Several such buildings were commissioned in Shanghai. The style utilized Western structural techniques on to which was grafted Chinese ornamentation. Critics called it "pigtail" architecture because of its attempt to add Chinoisserie feeling to Western structures.

Fine Chinese art is unfortunately almost impossible to find in Chinatown today. Antique vases, and scrolls can be seen in the museums and sometimes purchased at auctions from art dealers outside of Chinatown, but the embargo against mainland China stopped the flow of such pieces into the United States twenty years ago. Since then there has been only a trickle and such pieces as are to be found are expensive.

One of the finest and most important forms of Chinese art which is ubiquitous in any Chinatown but not recognized as such by a casual visitor is calligraphy. Painting and calligraphy are the highest forms of art in China, requiring the same material, brushes and ink and the same kind of dexterity. Calligraphy is the one form of art which is appreciated by all Chinese people even if they know nothing about art or literature. In childhood, they learned how to write by copying fine calligraphy with tracing paper until they had learned the technique of using the Chinese brush. The test of good calligraphy is in its execution, balance, structure, and rhythm. Chiang Yee, in his book *Chinese Calligraphy*, says, "Each character has a stable stance, with a gesture of movement, and the center of gravity falls upon the base. If any part of any character had been wrongly placed, the whole would have appeared to totter." The characteristic which is looked for has also been called "rhythmic vitality" in the strokes. Each character, or ideograph as it is called, represents an idea. Although most of the shopkeepers in Chinatown are not well educated, they appreciate good calligraphy and feel that having it on their store signs will bring them good fortune. It is not surprising therefore, that the most popular use of calligraphy is in store signs.

Chinese newspaper stands or bookstores display a number of Chinese language newspapers published in America, magazines published in Formosa and Hong Kong, and soft-bound novels, short stories, and novelettes. There are over ten Chinese newspapers published in the United States, one of which is in both English and Chinese. Magazines that look like Chinese versions of *Life, Look, Time,* and *Newsweek* are particularly popular. For the male-dominated oversea Chinese population, these magazines particularly highlight attractive Hong Kong movie starlets.

The availability of such literary enjoyment for non-scholarly readers was the result of the literary revolution in 1917 started by Dr. Hu Shih (1891–1962). Prior to this time, written Chinese was a scholars' medium with a very complicated and highly stylized prose. The literary revolution brought about a written language which followed colloquial speech.

The Cantonese opera, unfortunately, is now only rarely performed, even in the large Chinatowns. A grand spectacle of fine silk costumes and magnificent head-pieces, this stylized performance portrayed ancient China. The demand for this entertainment was not great enough to justify its continuance and the opera singers and musicians have found economic refuge in the restaurant business. Occasionally, during Chinese festivals and holidays, the opera is played.

Chinese music can be heard in Chinatown on records or tapes, in some juke boxes and in New York City on FM radio. Based on the pentatonic or five tone scale, it may sound disonant to the Western ear. It does not have harmony or counterpoints and is composed of melody, rhythm, and form. Music also plays a part in the Chinese language which has been described so often as being singsongish. Chinese is monosyllabic and each mono-syllable is expressed, in musical terms, in a rising, falling, or level melodic movement. The same monosyllable, if uttered in a different tone conveys a different meaning. It should be added here, that this does not mean that Chinese cannot be "tone-deaf" which has to do with pitch rather than tonal movement.

Chinese-speaking films imported mainly from Hong Kong are made chiefly to please the taste of Chinese in Southeast Asia. On the whole, the quality of acting and production is poor. It is melodramatic and still many years away from becoming an art form. There are generally no English subtitles.

Ivory carvings, imported from Hong Kong, can be found in Chinatown, but one must be careful to differentiate between ivory and bone which is much cheaper. Canton was for a long time the center of this little industry which was considered a craft rather than art.

Genuine tomb pieces such as pottery horses, camels, and other figurines are rare, but fairly inexpensive copies can be found from time to time. The tomb pieces are symbols of servants substituted for actual servants who were, in ancient times, buried with their masters to care for them after death. The use of Ming-chi (burial figurines and models) started probably as early as the Shang Dynasty (1766? or 1523–1028 B.C.) and continued for many hundreds of years. The copies which can be found are of porcelain horses and camels of the T'ang period (A.D. 618–967).

The center of the jade industry was also in Canton. The Chinese consider jade to be the most valuable of stones. In prehistoric times it was used to make useful articles. It was during the Ch'in (221–206 B.C.) and Han (206 B.C.–A.D. 221) dynasties that it began to be used for decorative purposes. It is reputed to have medicinal value and, powdered, has been used as an ingredient in remedies for kidney ailments. Although the Chinese in America do not use it as a medicine, its value as a talisman against disease and accident is considered great. The term "jade" covers several minerals, chiefly nephrite and jadeite. As originally formed in nature they are white (and sometimes still found in this pure state) but through some chemical process change over the centuries to green, red, brown, lavender, and black. Green jade is commonly used for jewelry, the most prized being emerald green. Jade rings, necklaces and earrings can be purchased in Chinatown jewelry stores.

Fifty years ago, when the Chinese in America still were clinging to their queues, their robes, and their language, one knew immediately that here was "little China." Fortunately, or unfortunately, their practices have changed. Men wear business suits. Only a few of the women, particularly those who were born in China, wear Chinese dresses.

The truth is that they are all becoming Americanized whether they like it or not. Even older men have their commitment to this country, many having become citizens and brought their families here. In Arizona, the Chinese have spread out and one finds men in their late sixties speaking English without an accent. They approach life as any American would. They have, however, made an effort to hold onto some of their heritage by forming a Chinese community center where the Chinese language can be taught so that their children and grandchildren do not entirely lose their heritage. It is doubtful that they can succeed. Children everywhere are determined to conform to their surroundings. Why should they attend Chinese school every day when their friends are out playing? What is the need for the Chinese language, they ask? This evolution is taking place in other Chinese communities. The only place which might remain Chinese for a long period of time is San Francisco where new immigrants arrive with language and ancient customs still intact.

Chinatown business has continuously adjusted to American ways. Even the grocery stores are now well equipped with stainless steel and glass store fronts. Packaging and merchandising have been Americanized. There are even Chinese supermarkets in San Francisco and New York. Chinese New Year is becoming the occasion for public relations and publicity for Chinatown as well as a holiday for the Chinese. Gaudy drum majorettes and brass bands are beginning to drown out the drums of the dragon boys. Soon, perhaps, the dragons themselves will be gone.

It is still possible for a person to live in Chinatown without ever having to go outside it. All of his needs can be taken care of through the Chinese stores and his whole social life through the clans. But, the body of non-English speaking people is now very small. It is conve-

nient for the Chinese-American housewife to live near
Chinese grocery stores, as she still serves Chinese meals
once or twice a day. For the man who feels he must work
in Chinatown, he can do so only in the large cities where
the Chinatowns are both residential and business. Here,
families live in Chinatown because they do not want
their children to lose their cultural heritage completely.

One of the subjects most discussed by Chinese parents
is that of their children speaking Chinese. They have just
about given up trying to teach them how to write or even
to read Chinese characters. They also want them to be
aware of Chinese customs and attitudes. This usually
means a knowledge of filial piety and "face." But their
American children find this the most difficult of all. Even
the parents today are ignorant of Chinese philosophy—
Confucianism, Buddhism, or Taoism, and only a few of
the gods, such as the Kitchen God, are thought of by any
Chinese-American, and only in the way American children think of Santa Claus. But all Chinese parents want
to be sure that their children marry a Chinese.

Chinatown is also a changing America. You will meet
immigrants working in the restaurants, the grocery
stores, and curio shops. You will see the housewife buying Chinese groceries, but her children won't know a
word of Chinese. You will find in a few old stores a
touch of the ancient past where nothing is familiar, but
you will see modernized stores ready and eager to do
business with the American clientele.

The change is not just external. It is not only that neon
lights replace the old wooden signs with carved characters. It is the change in the ways of the people living
and working there. Soon there may be no Chinatowns at
all. If you want to witness these most exotic fragments
of the past, go now.

CHAPTER 10

Chinatown, West

After the San Francisco fire of 1906, Will Irwin, one of the first writers to appreciate the beauty of Old China-town, wrote:

> It is gone—gone with the sea-gray city which encircled it. The worse order changeth, giving place to the better; but there is always so much in the worse order which our hearts would have kept! In a newer and stronger San Francisco rises a newer, cleaner, more beautiful Chinatown. Better for the city, oh, yes! and better for the Chinese, who must come to modern ways of life and health if they are to survive among us. But . . . where is the dim reach of Ross Alley, that horror to the nose, that perfume to the eye? Where are those broken dingy streets in which the Chinese made an art of rubbish.

If one can ever be thankful for a disaster, here indeed is such a situation. If it were not for the fire of 1906 San Francisco might never have had the most charming Chinatown in the country. Not the artificial contrived type built in Los Angeles but a place where Chinese live, work, and play, a place which has a "lived-in" feel, adding to its culture and beauty, San Francisco's Chinatown feels the pulse of the metropolis. But, being on the Western shores and the largest port for newcomers to the New World from the Orient, it is always replenished with new immigrants and thus never completely loses the charm of the way of the Old Country.

The north end of San Francisco's Chinatown, at Grand and Broadway, is where the Chinese live and shop. As early as 1854 the area from Washington Street to Sacramento along the east side of DuPont (now called Grant) and the alleys of this vicinity were spoken of as "little China." Here the first Chinese merchants established their stores and teahouses. By 1877 it was six blocks in length running north and south on DuPont Street from California to Broadway, and two blocks wide from east to west on Sacramento, Clay, Commercial, Washington, Jackson, Pacific, and Broadway streets, from Kearney to Stockton, crossing DuPont.

On every side red and gilt greeted the eye. Large wooden signs with carved Chinese characters hung outside the places of business. Every nook and corner along the sidewalks was crowded by the stalls of curbstone merchants selling vegetables, fruits, and sweetmeats, and by specialists offering their services—cobblers, razor sharpeners, and tinkers, each occupying not more than two or three feet. Some of these paid a small rental, but many were free tenants. In some parts of Chinatown were cellars where the poorest and least fortunate Chinese lived.

For gifts such as lacquered boxes, vases, and ivory carvings one used to go to Chine Lee's on Kearney Street or King Tai's under the Palace Hotel or Lung's on Sacramento Street, between Montgomery and Kearney.

A "joss house" called the "Eastern Glorious Temple" was owned and run by Dr. Lai Bo Tai, a Chinese herb doctor. By the late 1870s there were two principal Chinese theaters, both on Jackson Street between Kearney and DuPont, where traditional Chinese plays depicting historical events were put on. Some old frame buildings were still standing by the 1870s. By and large the buildings were of plain American architecture but the theaters, the restaurants, the joss houses, and some other buildings were fancifully decorated and lit up with Chinese lanterns of all sizes and shapes that fluttered and flickered in front of all public places.

On Jackson Street was a silversmith, and men making finger rings, hairpins, and other Chinese ornaments. The Chinese nearly monopolized the manufacturing of overalls in California at one time and the work was done right on DuPont. Also to be found on this street were shirtmakers, a shoe factory, and a tin shop. Everywhere was a smell which was characteristic of Chinatown in the late 1800s. As described by Reverend O. Gibson it was ". . . the smell of cigars, and tobacco leaves wet and dry, dried fish and vegetables; all these toned to a certain degree by what may be called a shippy smell, produced a sensation upon the olfactory nerves of the average American."

This area from California Street to Broadway, the birthplace of Chinatown, is now the "little China" within Chinatown. Look carefully and you will still find some of the old pioneer firms. There is Wo Kee at Grant Avenue, established in 1856 as a supplier of food and clothing to the early Chinese miners. A store specializing in Chinese slippers at 857 Grant, has survived over a hundred years. Quong Lee, a general mercantile store, was established in 1865 as a men's clothing shop. At the corner of Washington Street and Wentworth Place since 1880 is Tuck Hing, the first poultry and meat market in Chinatown. Tai Hing Lung, importer-exporter, is still being managed by the family who founded it in 1885.

All over the north end of Grant Avenue the storekeepers each morning lay out their fresh meats, fish, and vegetables for eager Chinese housewives who come to buy their provisions for the day. Freshly roasted ducks, squabs, chicken, suckling pigs are hung in the store windows. For the busy housewife some stores even have prepared vegetables and other vegetables ready to be eaten. Among these shoppers are some old women with their hair tied back in a bun, wearing black Chinese dresses and walking in a way which indicates that their feet were bound in childhood.

Watch the salesmen, each equipped with a long blue apron, giving individual attention to their customers. Watch them add up the bill on an abacus seemingly as quickly as an IBM machine might do it.

Chinatown is not immune to change imposed by the modern age. Interspersed throughout this colorful district are some elaborate stainless steel and glass store fronts and self-service supermarkets dealing in Chinese goods. Though Chinese herbs and spices are lined up in the shelves, at the end of the line is not an abacus but an automatic cash register, in shiny contrast to the warm dark wooden storefronts of the tiny grocery stores with bamboo baskets filled with Chinese vegetables. The large carved wooden signs with gilded Chinese characters are being replaced by neon lights and aluminum even at this end of "little China."

The casual observer may not know that these stores have taken the place of the large industries which once occupied this end of town. Gone are the cigar factories, the shoe factories, and the furniture factories. Gone are the merchants' stalls above which hung narrow boxes to which with the help of a stepladder the storekeeper climbed and slept in. Can one really regret their departure? Not only has the appearance of Chinatown changed, new business and new professions have been added. The four-story signs of the large and flourishing savings and loan associations prominently light up the whole north end of Grant Avenue. Here is the secret of the Chinese. Their thriftiness and wise investment in real estate has tided them over good and bad times. Also found in this area in the new office buildings are insurance brokers, travel agencies, real estate companies, medical, dental, legal and accounting services, many of them run by second and third generation Chinese-Americans. These changes have taken place only since World War II.

In this neighborhood also are hardware stores where one can purchase a *wok*, a large round pan for cooking, and a *choy doh*, the famous Chinese cleaver. Clothing stores, some of them with unlikely Chinese names such as Winky's Children's Shop and Kaye's Footwear Store, are indications of the changing order.

Don't miss a chance to visit one of the herb shops which also line this area. In the windows you will see dried deer antlers and sea horses from Hong Kong. Inside the store are drawers which cover all the walls. Each drawer contains a different herb. A strange medicinal smell will penetrate your nostrils. Although many old timers still go to herb doctors these apothecaries no longer do a thriving business since there are now about fifty Chinese MD's in the area. You may want to go into one of them to buy some spices, fine flavored powder or star anis, for your barbecue or Chinese cooking at home and have the experience of watching the man carefully weigh it on a delicate hand scale. Hold your breath or you may blow some of it off.

Two blocks to the north of this Chinese shopping area is a Chinese housing project in which over four hundred families live. It is called Ping Yuen, the "Tranquil Gardens." The buildings are unmistakenly Chinese as indicated by the second floor balconies which are decorated with designs of Chinese figures and characters.

Only a block to the south of the housing project off Jackson and Stockton is the Chinese hospital, the only Chinese operated one in the United States. Erected in 1924, it has sixty beds, is staffed by both Orientals and Occidentals and serves all people regardless of race or religion. It is supported by the contributions of the local community.

While you are on Jackson Street you should find out for yourself why the Chinese call this street "Jeweler's Row." The favorite gems are jade, opal, and pearl, with jade very far out in front. These craftsmen will make intricate solid gold jewelry on request. Mr. Sam Choy, the proprietor of the Wung Fat Company at 749 Jackson Street for thirty years, is perhaps typical of the jewelers of Jackson Street. The items in his store which include rings, earrings, pins, pendants, figurines, and jade bead necklaces range in price from $25 to $5000. But, like the other jewelers who love the business, he is not too anxious to sell his valuable and beautiful pieces to just anyone. Unless he is convinced that the customer is able to appreciate an especially fine piece, it will not be for sale at any price. This is especially true if it is a fine bit of jade. To get Sam, or any other jeweler on Jackson Street to part with, or even to show you, a valuable jade you had better be prepared to spend some time winning his friendship and convincing him that you will take good care of his very prized possession.

While on Jackson Street you should take a peek at the site of sin where, in the old days, wine, women, and song played havoc with the morals of men. It is at Jason Court between Grant and Stacton. The Chinese called it *"Gum Gook Yuen Hong,"* Lane of Golden Chrysanthemums.

Across the way, connecting Jackson with Washington, is Ross Alley which used to be called "Old Spanish Alley" (*Gow Louie Sung Hong*). In the early days, Ross Alley and Spofford Alley, called "New Spanish Alley" (*Sun Louie Sung Hong*), were much frequented by Mexicans and Spaniards who patronized the gambling establishments on them.

Old Chinatown Lane, off Washington Street, and Ross and Spofford Alleys, are used for motion picture and television locations when shooting scenes which feature intrigue, opium, and the general clichés of vice. But don't expect to find these things if the Hollywood producers are not on hand to pay for the performance. Old Chinatown Alley had the Chinese name of *Mar Tong Hong* "Horse Stable Alley" because it used to be the site of stables. It formerly had the name of Church Street and later, Cameron Alley.

At Spofford and Washington is the small Kwan Yin Temple for those who wish to pay tribute to the goddess of mercy. It houses a larger-than-life-size image of Kwan Yin, reputed to have been carved during the end of the Sung Dynasty (A.D. 959–1178).

The Tin Hau Temple on Waverly place, a Taoist Temple, contains a gold covered main altar with the image of Tin Hou, the Queen of Heaven, and the protectress of travelers and seafarers. The temple was built in 1875 in gratitude for the safe voyage of the early immigrants across the Pacific. It is maintained by the Sue Hing Benevolent Association.

Nearby are a number of schools. Particularly striking is the Nan Kue School building, patterned after a Mandarin courthouse, with a pair of stone lions guarding the upper story. The roof is topped with glazed tiles and painted eaves. The school is supported by the Nan Hoy Association which uses the main hall as a meeting room.

San Francisco's Chinatown has more than half a dozen large Chinese language schools, with ten smaller ones scattered throughout the city. Their curriculum consists of reading, writing, history, geography, general science, with literature and Chinese-English translation in the upper grades. There are approximately four thousand students enrolled in these schools, attending two-hour classes, in addition to classes in American schools.

One of the sightseeing spots of San Francisco's Chinatown is the Chinese telephone central office at 743 Washington Street. This lovely little building with its three-pagoda roof designed completely in the Chinese style once housed the unique exchange of the Pacific Telephone Company which serviced the Chinatown area with operators fluent in both English and Chinese. The operators of the old "China–5" exchange knew the names, addresses, phone numbers, and living habits of the over two thousand subscribers and could locate a person at any time of the night or day. This operation has been closed since 1949 when it gave way to the system of dial telephones.

The north end of Grant Avenue, the "little China" of the nineteenth century, is still the goal of the newly arrived immigrant. Here he feels most secure, where everyone on the street speaks his language, and the storekeepers understand what he wants. Here are all the necessities of life from birth to death. At this end of Chinatown can be found a unique way of life, not to be found anywhere else in the United States.

Having observed some of the Chinese at work and play and some of the historic spots you will want to visit the other end of Grant Avenue. Its entrance way is at Bush and Grant. In these stores are still a few very beautiful pieces of antiques and jewelry which one can purchase in America, but they can be purchased only if the proprietor is willing. The salesman will be eager, as a matter of fact anxious, to sell you some inexpensive souvenirs of your visit made in Japan, Formosa, or Hong Kong. But, if you are interested in something better, then do it on a day when you have plenty of time to chat with the salesman and convince him that you are truly interested in Chinese art.

Red, gold and green dragon-entwined lampposts and the sound of tinkling brass temple bells hung from the pagoda topped lamps greet the visitor as he enters Chinatown from its gateway on Grant Avenue and Bush.

The first block, that is the 400 block on Grant, has shops featuring Hong Kong teakwood furniture in contemporary design or copies of antiques. A few old pieces may be found if you look hard enough. The City of Hankow Tassel Company, on this first block, has, among other things, brassware, furniture, lamps, ivory carvings, lacquerware, screens, and scrolls.

Walking east on Pine Street you will find St. Mary's Park, a lovely place to rest your feet. In the center of the park stands an unusual statue of Dr. Sun Yat-sen, founder and first president of the Chinese Republic. Created by sculptor Benjamino Bufano, the statue stands twelve feet high, is of stainless steel with head and hands of rose-colored granite. If you happen to be in the park when school is out don't be too shocked if you find Chinese children using this memorial of China's George Washington as home base in punch ball.

To the east of St. Mary's Park is Kong Chow Temple, the oldest temple in San Francisco, maintained by people from the Kong Chow district in Kwangtung, China. The temple is dedicated to Kwan Ti (or Kwan Kung), god of valor and loyalty, who is the patron of soldiers, and all whose pursuits are of a hazardous nature. There are several classrooms on the ground floor for the teaching of the Confucian classics. The temple is open to the public.

Back on the 500 block of Grant Avenue you will find some of the most exquisite *objets d'art*, if you have the time to win the trust of the storekeepers who have hidden away the last few prized antiques. If they are for sale at all they must be sold to the proper person, someone who will appreciate them. The House of Sung at 527 Grant Avenue may seem like only a bookshop at first glance but if you get to know Mr. Fung you will discover why this modest little shop is known for its oriental art objects and antiques.

Mr. Fung, a soft spoken self-educated man, gingerly unwraps each precious piece and stands back to let its

beauty speak for itself. It may take a second or third
visit to win his confidence but soon enough he will show
you the antique porcelains and earthenware from the
Han Dynasty, vases from the Ming, Sung and Ch'in dynasties, none of which he is anxious to sell. Perhaps you
might find a Chinese print or a book which he would be
willing to part with.

At Mane On at 550 Grant Avenue some very fine pieces
of porcelain can be found. In contrast to Mr. Fung, one
of the proprietors of this establishment has memorized a
short lecture on porcelains to be delivered to tourists. He
is mainly interested in pushing the commercial mass-pro-
duced items, but be firm and maybe he will show you the
Kang-si, Ming, Chien lung porcelains that are kept on
his second floor.

Bolts of brocade silks, embroidered linen, and laces are
displayed by the City of Shanghai where you may also
have a *cheong-sam* (a Chinese dress) made to order.

As you approach the 600 block you will be struck by
the blending of the sounds and sights of Chinatown with
the famous bright yellow cable car clanging its way
along California Avenue. The brassy clang and the people hanging on the car's side rails add to the festive atmosphere of your trip. At the corner of Grant and California is a restaurant with balconies overlooking this
wonderful sight and you will want to make a mental note
to dine there for an atmospheric if not a delicious dinner.

Old St. Mary's Church called Dai Choong Low, the
"Tower of the Big Bell," by the Chinese at California
and Grant was once the Catholic Cathedral of San Francisco. It was erected in 1854 of stone brought from China
and brick from New England. A tourist guide will
proudly point out the first Chinese motif outdoor telephone booth, which by the way has been copied by New
York's Chinatown. Several shops on this block specialize
in rattanware and tableware.

When you arrive at Sacramento Street you will have reached Tang Yun Gai, or the "Street of the Men of Tang." This was the street where in the 1850s the Chinese vendors sold their wares.

If you are now ready for dinner, you happen to be right in the middle of the restaurant area. San Francisco's Chinatown is filled with good eateries for every taste and pocketbook with menus ranging from ham and eggs to fifteen-course Chinese banquets. For a cup of coffee or tea and a light snack or a place to rest one's feet there are any number of coffee shops on the north side of Grant Street and along the side streets. Drop in at Ping Yuen Bakery and Coffee Shop at 1026 Grant near Jackson for a *char shui bow*, steamed bun filled with roast pork and a juicy sauce, or at Fong Fong Bakery for almond cookies, sesame seed cookies, custard tarts and other baked goods.

For lunch the Chinese usually have *dim sum* (described in Chapter 8) or noodles either in soup with meats and vegetables or sautéed, or rice congee.

Yank Sing at the corner of Powell and Broadway is a little out of the way and not a very good-looking place but their *har gow* (shrimp dumplings) and *fun quor* are the best in San Francisco and probably the best in the United States. They look and taste like the best that is served in the teahouses of Hong Kong. This is a family business operated with the help of the teenage sons and daughters. If the table is a little greasy don't waste your time trying to get a waiter to clean it up, just wipe it up with the paper napkins on the table and stop the waiter as he runs by you with a tray full of an assortment of *dim sum*. You may order a particular blend of tea if you wish such as Jasmine, Chrysanthemum, dragon well or simply get a potful of Oolong or red tea. Every once in a while the waiter will carry out of the kitchen a round bamboo steamer filled with something freshly made.

Nearby at Powell and Broadway is a little hole in the wall run by a lady chef who also serves *dim sum* and in addition has an assortment of noodle dishes. A very popular teahouse is the Hang Ah Tea Room at 1 Hang Ah Street near the playground. Also there is the Songhay Tea House at 650 Jackson. *Dim sum* is served only during the lunch hours from 11 A.M. to 2 P.M.

Another place which you should not miss is Wo Kee on Washington Street near Wentworth where you walk through the kitchen to a flight of stairs which takes you to the dining rooms on the second and third floors. This place is famous for its rice congee and noodle dishes. The hours are odd and a carryover from those of the traditional noodle houses of China. You will be welcome from 11 A.M. to 2 P.M. and then not until 5:30. If you don't go at the right hours no amount of pleading with the chefs resting on the street will gain entrance for you.

For dinner you also have a great number of choices. If you have been "slumming" all day you may wish to dine elegantly at the Imperial Palace . . . beautifully decorated with Chinese antiques placed in a dramatic setting. It has superb waiter service, frankly a rarity in Chinese restaurants, each course served on your plate with great dexterity and style. The specialty of the house is Beef Imperial, sliced sirloin sautéed with snow peas, water chestnuts, bamboo shoots, mushrooms, and garnished with crispy deep fried rice noodles which melt in your mouth.

Displayed at Tao Tao Restaurant at 675 Jackson Street are thirty-three enlarged reproductions of Arnold Genthe's famous photographs of Old Chinatown. Tao Tao's extensive menu ranges from family dinners to very special dishes which must be ordered in advance. This restaurant can boast that it has the best banquet chefs in the business. If you would like their cooking at its best, join with six or ten others, phone a day or two in advance, give the head chef carte blanche, and experience the adventure of a Chinese banquet.

Nam Yuen at 740 Washington Street is filled every evening (except Monday when it is closed) with a mixture of Chinese and American customers. Its bar is too crowded to allow you to be comfortable but the food is a superb example of home cooking.

The best and most famous of Peking cooking, the duck bearing the name of this beautiful city, is served at the Tao Yuen Restaurant. The crispy, crackling skin is eaten with steamed buns, and the meat, well seasoned and succulent is eaten with rice or noodles. Also serving food of Northern China is the Four Seas which has as its specialities Szechuan Fragrant Duck and Peking Crackling Soup.

If you want to rub elbows with movie celebrities and get the "red carpet" treatment you must dine at Kan's. One can hardly go wrong in San Francisco's Chinatown. Other famous restaurants are Cathay House, Far East, Good Earth, Great Eastern, Kuo Wah and Shanghai Low, just to name a few.

If the pocketbook is low and the sense of adventure is high, don't ever be afraid to try the small basement places on the side streets.

Los Angeles' New Chinatown could only happen in the city which produced Hollywood. Garish, flaming with pastel colors and neon lights, it is the "Disneyland" of Chinatowns in the U.S.A. It is advertised as the most beautiful, clean, and attractive in the United States. It is the only one built from the ground up in Oriental spirit and architecture. Although a few families live on Mei Ling Way above the shops, and some children may be found playing handball at Mei Ling and Gin Ling Way, the New Chinatown is not lived in. Nevertheless, it is fun to visit the area built after the pattern of Peking's forbidden city.

Los Angeles is an important spot in the history of the Chinese in America. Its first Chinese inhabitant, a servant of Joseph Newmark, arrived in 1854. By 1861 there were twenty-one men and eight women, most of them working in five or six laundries and some of them working as cooks and servants. The people of Los Angeles were stirred up when a Chinese came from San Francisco to open what he called a "curiosity shop" carrying an assortment of Chinese goods and articles which the people of Los Angeles had never seen before.

From 1861 onward the Chinese population started to grow in and around the area known as Nigger Alley.

In October 1871, twenty-two Chinese were lynched in Los Angeles, one of the worst massacres in the history of the Chinese in America. The facts are difficult to piece together accurately. Newspaper accounts of the time say that a "war" broke out on October 21 near Nigger Alley between two Chinese factions apparently over a woman who was forcibly abducted by one of the groups. The fight resulted in several arrests and the battle was ended. However, the next day it started up again and when the police and some white citizens tried to break it up, one policeman was wounded and a white citizen killed.

News of the resistance to arrest spread through Los Angeles so fast that by nightfall hundreds of white citizens armed with guns, pistols, ropes, and knives had surrounded Nigger Alley and Spring Street to avenge the white man's death. They grabbed all of the Chinese in sight and hung them on the corral gates all over the neighboring streets wherever they happened to have been caught. Twenty-two Chinese were killed by the end of the night. The verdict of the coroner's jury was "death through strangulation by persons unknown to the jury." Only the bodies were in evidence. No one testified.

The Chinese government made a formal protest about the treatment of its nationals and eventually received an indemnity.

In 1876 Chinese workers finished boring the San Fernando tunnel for the extension of the Southern Pacific Railroad to Los Angeles. With the railroad finished, many Chinese laborers worked on the farms in Southern California particularly in the San Joaquin Valley. It was the Chinese who made a success of the celery industry and California's fruit business would have been delayed for decades had it not been for Chinese labor.

From farming some enterprising Chinese went into the produce brokerage business. City Market became a joint distribution point for the Chinese produce merchants. Today there are over twenty-five Chinese firms in the produce business here.

The City Market area, in the vicinity of South San Pedro and East Ninth streets, is a good place to eat because the restaurants cater to the Chinese residents and businessmen. The Man Fook Low Restaurant, at 962½ South San Pedro Street, and New Moon Café, at 914 South San Pedro Street, both specialize in *dim sum*.

At one time, Old Chinatown covered the area bounded by Los Angeles, Alison, Alameda streets and Sunset Boulevard. This was demolished to make room for the new Union Station and with the demolition went the old dilapidated quarters which dated back to Spanish times. Even before Old Chinatown was torn down a second Chinese settlement was located in the North Spring Street area through North Main from Macy to Ord streets. This section, though old and quite run down, is still inhabited by Chinese and is where most of them buy Chinese goods.

All of the other Chinatowns look at Los Angeles' New Chinatown with envy because it is the only one which is totally owned and operated by the Chinese. When the plans for the demolition of Old Chinatown were announced in the 1930s a group of Chinese businessmen with the leadership of Peter Soo-Hoo joined to build a new and beautiful Chinatown.

This ambitious project was completed in June 1938. The architecture and color of New Chinatown is an attempt to reproduce the streets and temples in Peking City. The entranceway at the east gate on North Broadway is a colorful archway called the Pailou of Maternal Virtue. At the west gate is another archway of camphor wood with the inscription, *"The best things Chinese are gathered here."*

The completion of the transcontinental railroad, the reclamation of the swamps of California, and the finishing of the ditches for irrigation, the beginnings of Kearneyism (that is, the policy of driving Chinese laborers out by violence if necessary), race riots, and license taxes, marked the end of an era for the Chinese in America.

The early immigrants recruited for the development of the frontier west of the Mississippi, especially those in the Western and Rocky Mountain states, California, Washington, Oregon, Nevada, Utah, Idaho, Montana, Colorado, and Wyoming, left their settlements, many of them for the "old country," many of them for the East. So it happened that while the rest of the country was moving westward with the new railroads, the Chinese were going in the opposite direction. They left behind them little "Chinatowns" which had served the special needs of the mining, railroad, and ranching camps where Chinese had been employed.

Such a Chinese village was "Hong Kong" which flourished in the 1880s near the settlement of Manzanita in the state of Washington. It was reputed to have a population of three thousand Chinese but this is doubtful.

During anti-Chinese riots in many Puget Sound cities, the settlement was abandoned in such great haste that many pigs were left behind to find a warm welcome in some of the kitchens of the white settlers who followed.

In 1880 Oregon was second only to California in Chinese population with 3300. Most of the Chinese in Oregon and the State of Washington engaged in the fishing industry. The Chinese introduced the purse seine in 1886 which came to be employed in deep waters, especially after the appearance of the gasoline-powered boat equipped with winches to close and raise the seine when filled. Fishing gear up to this time represented in large measure development of the reef nets, basketwork, brush weirs, and traps employed for centuries by the Indians. Around the turn of the century, drastic changes occurred in fishing and packing. In 1903, E. S. Smith patented the "Iron Chink," so called because it replaced Chinese labor. The machine killed and cleaned sixty to eighty-five salmon a minute.

The Chinese population in Oregon today is relatively small with 2100 in the whole state of whom 1750 are in the city of Portland. There is a very small Chinatown in Portland occupying two or three streets with a few restaurants and a few Chinese grocery stores.

The State of Washington has a larger Chinese population (7000 according to the Chinese, less according to the official census) than has Oregon and it seems to be growing. The main street of the Chinese center in Seattle is King Street, running from Ninth to Maynard and across to Jackson on one side and Wellner on the other. The Chinese in Seattle were originally in the fishing business and some still work in the canneries. The area in which they live is not a tourist haunt. Located in a decaying part of the city and neighboring a Japanese and Negro area, Seattle's Chinatown is basically for the Chinese.

Chinese family associations and tongs take up several floors of the building on Ninth and King streets. The Chinese Benevolent Association has a fairly impressive building at Seventh Street and Wellner. An old bulletin board occasionally bears association notices but usually is covered with announcements of the next Chinese movie coming to town.

Because it has remained genuinely Chinese, rather than become a Chinatown for tourists, it is still possible to get good Chinese food here. Chinese restaurants are dotted throughout Seattle although most of them are fairly small. Rice congee and noodles are served at the Three Grand Restaurant at 664 S. King. The Tai Tung at the corner of Maynard and King serves *dim sum* every day at noon. The Chinese also eat at the Lin Yen, the Don Ting, and the Hong Kong. Chinese groceries may be bought at Kwan On Wing Company at 679 S. King and the Wa Sang Groceries at 663 S. King.

The unusual aspect of the Chinese settlement in Seattle is that Chinatown is becoming increasingly a place of business and not a place of residence. This is in contrast particularly to the Chinatowns of San Francisco and New York where the Chinese population live. The change began to take place during World War II when the Chinese in the restaurant businesses became more affluent and started to move to Beacon Hill. When the Japanese were relocated from Seattle during the war many Chinese bought up real estate and businesses of the Japanese. This may be a reason why Chinese-owned American grocery stores started outside of Chinatown. There are now at least several dozen grocery stores ranging from small to supermarkets. Beacon Hill today has so many Chinese and Japanese residents that it is called "Rice Paddy Hill" by the local Chinese and Japanese.

Although a Chinese population has remained at Seattle and Portland, in other towns the Chinese have disappeared or their number has become very small. In Butte, Montana, Chinatown at one time occupied the single square formed by Main, Galend, Colorado, and Mercury streets and divided by China Alley. There were at least five restaurants owned and operated by the Chinese specializing in preparing miners' lunch pails and serving breakfast and dinner. Today this area is old and shabby and except for a single building with carved ornaments on its façade and one or two neon signs, there is no external evidence that the quarter is Chinese.

In Montana there is the story of George Washington Taylor, the Chinese foster son of the prominent Taylor family which owned the Sands and Taylor Cattle Company. He was adopted by Jesse F. Taylor when his mother died and when he grew up he was given a hundred cattle with which to develop his own herd. George Washington Taylor built up the Kingsbury Ranch which became one of the finest ranches in the state. He lived in Helena, Montana, until his death in 1945 at the age of eighty-six.

The Chinese shoemaker of Garden Valley, Eldorado County, was born in the province of Canton in 1846. He came originally in 1862 to mine gold and purchased a claim at Johntown with thirty others. When the mine failed to pay, he abandoned it to take a place in the home of a Mr. Borland, a shoemaker in the village. In 1871 he purchased the residence and business of Mr. Borland and became a successful shoemaker.

Weaverville, California, was the place of the Weaverville "war" which involved several hundred Chinese in a pitch-fork type battle between two clans. It was also the site of the oldest joss house in the United States, the Temple of the Clouds and Forest, a gift from Moon Lee, the sole descendant of the pioneer Chinese who helped to settle Weaverville.

The Weaverville war took place on "Five Cent Gulch,"

Weaverville. Its cause is obscure, but it is known that it involved sectional differences between two groups of Chinese from different districts of Canton Province. A declaration of war was made weeks ahead of time and the date, July 15, 1854, set for the battle. Local blacksmiths were engaged by each side to make traditional Chinese weapons such as double-handed swords seven feet long, lances with large hooks near the head, fork handles ten feet long, having three tined forks about fifteen inches across the points, shields two feet six inches long and about twenty inches wide made of inch pine covered with tin, and hand swords. One report of the battle said:

> On the afternoon of July 15th, 1854, the two factions assembled, one called the "small party" and numbering about one hundred and thirty, the other called the "large party" and numbering nearly four hundred, —their banners were flying, and the parties were ranged on opposite sides of the gulch. Much defiant language was used, and some slight maneuvers were made. At length the small party charged upon the large one, and amid shouts and cheers from many hundreds of Americans, who stood upon the hill side to witness the battle, the small party put the others to flight, capturing their flag as a trophy of war and killing eight of their opponents, losing but two on their own side. An excited Swede firing at random among the combatants was shot down by someone behind.

Many Chinese went to Idaho in the early days to work in the placer mines. As placer mining declined those who were not driven out went into laundries or truck gardening. The Chinese population in the whole state of Idaho today is little more than a hundred, leaving behind only the fable of China Sam. China Sam came to be known as the Mayor of Warren. Known as

the most honest man in Idaho, he became the custodian
of the town's property and morals. He was popular with
the housewives also because he chopped their wood for
them and was known as a good babysitter and nurse to
the sick.

The "melting pot" of Wyoming is Rock Springs, a coal
mining community of Russians, Greeks, Finns, Irish, Italians, Negroes, and Chinese. The Chinese laborers were
first hired to work in the coal mines in 1875 during a
labor strike. By 1885 the Chinese population in Rock
Springs had grown to 1200 and on September 2 of that
year a riot broke out which resulted in the killing of
thirty Chinese and the burning of Chinese property. The
state militia had to be called out in order to stop the
mob. According to a witness, over two thousand shots
were fired and every building in Chinatown was burned.
Some Chinese returned later on to open laundries and
restaurants but they no longer engaged in coal mining.

Evanston, Wyoming, had a joss house until 1922 when
it burned down. At one time over six hundred coal miners and railroad section hands lived in Evanston. Food
for the whole town was supplied by vegetable gardeners
and peddlers who worked what was thought to be un-
productive land by lifting water from the stream with
wheels.

China Mary, one of the earliest residents of Evanston's
Chinatown, died on January 13, 1939, at an age believed
to be somewhere between 104 and 110. She charged ten
cents for having her picture taken in native costume.
There are hardly any Chinese in Evanston today where,
at one time, a dragon one hundred feet long, the largest
in the country, was paraded on Chinese New Year's.
Forty men carried it as they danced to the music of
drums, cymbals, and gongs.

Although there are very few Chinese in Deadwood,
South Dakota, today the lower end of Main Street near

Siever is still called Chinatown. Some of the men were engaged in the usual Chinese occupations as laundrymen and restaurant keepers. Others were merchants and doctors who conformed to the American fashions except that they kept their queues. The women and girls adhered to native costumes. A Mrs. Wong was the last Chinese woman to raise a family in Deadwood. An opium pipe which belonged to her is on display at the Adams Memorial Hall. Also on display at the museum are pictures of a Chinese Hose Team of America which won the great "hub and hub" race in Deadwood on July 4, 1888, and of a Chinese Sunday school class and some of the teachers.

There are no Chinatowns today in the Southwest but there are sizable Chinese populations of over a thousand in Phoenix, Tucson, San Antonio, and Houston.

The first Chinese settlers of Tucson, Arizona, were three men of the Wong clan who arrived in 1860 to open a restaurant. Others followed soon thereafter, one of the best known being Jim Sam, who became known as the "Chinese Midas." Arriving in the territory of Arizona in 1865, Sam moved from town to town establishing a successful restaurant in each town. When he retired from the business to become a money lender he was supposed to be worth well over $100,000.

The building of the Southern Pacific Railroad across Arizona also brought with it a large group of Chinese laborers, the greatest influx into Tucson being in 1880 when the railroad in Arizona was completed. Tucson's Chinese population grew from twenty in 1870 to 1630 in 1880. Many of the railroad laborers who had accumulated some capital established laundries and grocery stores which served not only the white population but also the Indians.

It is reported that Law Tai You, who had originally

been recruited to work in a Sonora, Mexico, mine but became dissatisfied, planted the first Chinese vegetable garden in Tucson in 1878. A few years later a number of Chinese gardeners rented, leased, or squatted on land on the Silver Lake District on the east side of the Santa Cruz River.

The rising number of Chinese in the state stimulated hostility. By 1878 efforts to bring Chinese laborers to work in a Clifton mine were defeated. In 1886 a resolution forbidding the employment of "coolies" in the place of white laborers was adopted by the Republican Territorial Convention in Tucson.

Tucson's small Chinatown located in an area in the triangle of Main, Pennington, and Pearl streets and along Alameda Street, was started around 1880. Construction of Tucson's City Hall later obliterated it. Chinese grocerymen of Tucson had to contend with thieves and murderers who plundered the area and escaped to the safety of the Sonora country. In an effort to protect themselves the Chinese merchants started the Tucson Chinese Chamber of Commerce. Even today this organization offers rewards of $100 to $500 for the capture of thieves, and $1000 to $2000 for the apprehension of a murderer.

Don Chum Wah, a cook for the Southern Pacific crews, one of the pioneers of Tucson, died in 1962 at the age of ninety-five. Having saved enough money to bring his wife over from China, he left his railroad job and they started a bakery business together and later expanded their project to include several markets. Most of their customers were Mexican and Indian and the two enterprising pioneers learned to speak those languages as well as English. Mrs. Don Wah found time to raise ten children, nine girls and one boy.

With the history of racial prejudice far behind them, the Chinese people of Arizona have, on the whole, done better financially and socially than any of their country-

men in America. Tucson and Phoenix have the most interesting of Chinese communities. The Chinese here,
both immigrants and native-born alike, have been assimilated into the American way of life and are accepted
as Americans. Financially, they have done very well. Until the end of World War II they controlled the lion's
share of the grocery business. Today the Chinese in
Tucson own 114 grocery stores, seven restaurants, seven
liquor stores, and sixteen other businesses. Many in both
Tucson and Phoenix, who invested wisely in real estate
have done exceedingly well with the fantastic growth of
these two cities. There are twenty Chinese-American
teachers in the Tucson school system and two Chinese
professors at the University of Arizona.

In Phoenix the Chinese own seventeen restaurants and
157 grocery stores. Wing F. Ong was the first Chinese
to have been elected to the state legislature. Thomas
Tang has served on the City Council and is now a judge.
His wife Dr. Pearl Tang is the County Health Officer of
Phoenix. John Sing Tang, a well-known architect, has
planned several of the schools in this city.

In sharp contrast to the assimilated communities of
Phoenix and Tucson is San Antonio, Texas, an old city
with a population more than half of whom are Mexican.
The Chinese workers on the Southern Pacific Railroad
came across San Antonio in their work and a few stayed.
By 1916 only two families were left, but in 1917 General
John J. Pershing brought back with him from Mexico
four hundred Chinese workers. He had found them running away from Pancho Villa and he had put them to
work for him. One of their tasks was to build Fort Sam
Houston. After that most of them opened grocery stores
and small shops. The original four hundred were made
citizens of the United States by a Congressional act
and many of them went back to China to bring over

their wives and children. About twenty of these original four hundred Chinese are still living in San Antonio.

Many of the first Chinese stores were in the western section of town around Santa Rosa Avenue. This section today is a very slummy dilapidated old Mexican neighborhood. Looking up Santa Rosa Avenue one sees some modern hotels and office buildings. But looking around one feels as though the clock has been turned back fifty or more years in a backward Mexican town. Wooden frame buildings and narrow congested streets make the parking meters look out of place. Bars, a chop suey cafe, saloons, bakeries making tortillas, and general stores occupy the first floors while the storekeepers have their homes on the second floor.

In this area are still a few Chinese although it cannot be called a Chinatown. Mr. and Mrs. Sam Gee run the general market on Santa Rosa. Mr. Gee and his family were raised right above the store although they no longer live there. This is generally the custom today. Most Chinese storekeepers have moved their homes away to better living quarters while keeping their stores where they were. Two tongs, the On Leong and Hip Sing Association, have club houses in this community. There is a Chinese school building which once housed fifty students, but which has not been used as a school for years. A general store selling Chinese groceries, dry goods, and other items is on Laredo Street. Some people buy their Chinese goods from a house-to-house peddler.

The Chinese population in San Antonio numbers about a thousand to fifteen hundred. By and large the community has tried to keep some of their traditional ways. They are probably the most conservative and most traditional of the Chinese in the U.S.A. Weddings are celebrated with Chinese banquets at the Chinese school and to these functions are invited almost the whole Chinese population of San Antonio. Wedding cakes are sent in from San Francisco for the occasion. When a baby is one month old, the San Antonio Chinese celebrate with the traditional red colored eggs and pickled ginger. Chinese New Year's and other holidays are celebrated with the prescribed food delicacies.

The Chinese organizations include the On Leong Tong, Hip Sing Tong, Kwok Ming Tang, and Chinese Free Masons, to which only the old-timers belong. There is also the Chinese Baptist Church and the Chinese American Citizens' Alliance (CACA). The Woman's Auxiliary of the CACA has a membership made up chiefly of American born Chinese. There is a Chinese Optimist's Club. The young married women get together for meetings and play Mah Jong. The men in the CACA bowl but the organization does not concern itself much with civic affairs.

The western part of town is to be torn down and rehabilitated soon. The people here are biding time. There are about 120 businesses of which eighty are groceries owned by Chinese in San Antonio. There is just one Chinese laundry.

The grocery stores are mainly the small general store type serving the Mexican population although some are in predominantly white communities. There are ten Chinese restaurants and one of the favorite places of the Chinese is Joy's. There are now a few professional people including a dentist, several engineers and an attorney.

Conservatively dressed and with her hair tied back in a bun, Mrs. Rose Wu might deceive you into thinking that she is one of the China-born matrons of the Chinese communities. This deception is quickly erased as she begins to speak perfect English with eloquence and vitality. She and her late husband Theodore Wu were leading citizens in the city of San Antonio and she is still so considered. Now the mother of three grown children, Mrs. Wu is the eldest daughter of pioneer Don Wah of Tucson. She and her sisters were the only single Chinese girls in the old days of Tucson. Delivering fresh bread with her father in a horse and carriage, warmed on the few chilly days of winter by the hot bricks under her seat, this daughter of a pioneer is a pioneer herself. Already in her youth she had become a courageous spokesman for the Chinese. Carrying herself with self-assurance, bouncing with energy, good-looking, and speaking eloquently she was listened to and respected.

Adventurous in spirit she and her husband Theodore moved to San Antonio to start a life of their own. Like other Chinese in that city they started in the grocery business but soon broadened their interests to the Tai Shan Restaurant, one of the nicest in the town. In 1937 Mrs. Wu testified before the Texas legislature against a bill which would have made it illegal for any alien to own property. Later she was sent by the mayor of San Antonio to represent the city in a good-will mission to South America. When Theodore Wu died in March 1961 the city hall of San Antonio was closed for one day in his honor.

The Chinese population in San Antonio is a stagnant one which has not increased in many years except for the natural increase through birth. Very few if any Chinese are coming to this city, a conservative community which has no industry and which supports itself on retired Army officers and nearby military bases.

In this environment where there are so many Mexicans who cling to their traditions, the Chinese are not stimulated to take on American ways. The atmosphere of San Antonio is not conducive to it and therefore San Antonio's Chinatown is one of the most interesting conservative Chinese communities in the U.S.A.

Houston, the largest city in the South, the sixth largest in the nation, is growing fantastically and so is its Chinese population. No one can really say when the first

Chinese arrived. In 1935 there were only about fifty. In 1960 there were approximately three thousand. With the growth of Houston itself, the Chinese of Houston also encouraged their friends and relatives to try their luck here where the depression did not hit hard. Many Chinese from Mississippi and Arkansas and even Chicago came to Houston and are still coming into this city.

Most of the China-born people are in the grocery business. There are approximately two hundred establishments ranging from large supermarkets to small stores serving Negro communities. There are only about ten Chinese restaurants. The Texans have not discovered Chinese food. The Chinese in Houston are proud of the fact that there is not a single Chinese laundry in that city.

As evidence of the older China-oriented group there is a Chinese Merchants' Association, the On Leong Association, which has its headquarters at 805 Charter Street. Here the members meet to settle their disputes and socialize. This building, decorated with eaves and pagoda tops and taking up half of a block, seems to be a waste of money since it is seldom used. It is nevertheless the symbol of the China-oriented group in this community.

The Chinese-Americans in Houston seem to have become well integrated with American society. Among the second-generation Chinese a few have gone to college and are now in the professions, though not all of them have stayed in Houston. In recent years almost all Chinese high school students have gone to college. In 1961 the "almost all" became "all" for every Chinese student in Houston who was graduated from high school that year went on to an institution of higher learning in the fall. As is becoming more and more true throughout America, the young Chinese in Houston do not speak Chinese.

The Chinese Baptist Church at 1823 Lamar Street conducts a school where children are taught how to read, write, and speak the language of their ancestors. There are about forty students and classes are held once a week. The Chinese in Houston live in private homes spread out throughout the city and therefore there is not much occasion for them to speak Chinese to each other. The church is one of the places of congregation where the Chinese can get together. Other organizations in Houston include the Chinese American Citizens' Alliance, the Gee's Family Association, the Gee Tuck Association, the On Leong Chinese Merchants' Association, and the Hip Sing Association. Most cities have a predominance of one family group or another and in Houston the predominant family group is the Gee family.

Whether or not Chinese banquets are held for weddings is usually some indication as to whether Chinese are still keeping up with their traditions. In Houston they seldom accompany a wedding. One of the problems probably is that there is a lack of good Chinese chefs in the city. According to the Chinese American Directory, published in 1950 by the Houston Lodge of the Chinese-American Citizens' Alliance, there are about fourteen Chinese restaurants. The largest and most plush is Albert Gee's Poly-Asian Restaurant located at 9530 South Main. Other restaurants are Lee's Den at 8100 South Main and Ming Palace at 2015 West Gray Street.

In Houston many of the American-born Chinese belong to the Chinese American Citizens' Alliance. The CACA was started many years ago in San Francisco as a lobby group which concerned itself with immigration problems and the poor treatment of the Chinese in America. The Houston Lodge started in 1954. Its membership consists of the second-generation Chinese Americans. There is also a Woman's Auxiliary of the CACA.

This organization has been able quietly in its own way

to put pressure on various bodies. Once a Chinese girl applied for a job at an oil company. She applied at the same time one of her classmates applied and her classmate, a white girl, was accepted but she was not. She insisted on an explanation and finally the woman told her that she was being turned down because she was Chinese. The members of the CACA quietly and without any publicity stopped buying gas from that company. Six months later the sales manager inquired why no Chinese had used his charge account for six months. After that, the oil company liberalized its employment policy so that Chinese were employed.

Another incident involved a statewide groceryman's association which prohibited anyone who was not white from becoming an officer. When this came out into the open all of the Chinese grocerymen resigned. The Association quickly changed its constitution and at present a Chinese is on the Board of Directors.

Chicago has the largest Chinese community in the Midwest. Its first settler was apparently T. C. Moy who lived at the corner of Clark and Van Buren streets in 1870. Today there are about seven thousand Chinese in Chicago of whom about two thousand live in Chinatown. The present Chinatown was established in 1923. It covers nearly a dozen square blocks and is bounded on the north by Archer Avenue, on the east by South LaSalle Street, on the south by West 24th Street, and on the west by Stewart Avenue. The era of first class Chinese restaurants in Chicago started as early as the 1890s and in the decades that followed they became very numerous within the Loop. No longer the gay nightlife spot of Chicago, Chicago's Chinatown still has some fine restaurants, gift shops, and grocery stores. The latter supply many restaurants located in the Midwest.

Chicago's Chinatown has many organizations, including among others the Chinese Consolidated Benevolent Association, the American Legion Post, Chinese Merchants' Association (On Leong Tong), the Hip Sing Association, Chinese-American Civic Council, the Chinese-American Citizens' Alliance, and the Chinese Women's Club.

Five hundred Chinese children go to the two schools in Chinatown which teach Chinese reading and writing, Chinese history, geography, and elocution, as well as painting and the use of the abacus.

Of interest to tourists to Chicago's Chinatown is the On Leong Tong building at 2216 Westworth Avenue which is a striking gold building with red pagoda tops and balconies. On the third floor is a room which is furnished like an American courtroom save that it is decorated with Chinese tapestries. This is called the Chinese city hall where disputes and problems are discussed and arbitrated. In the adjoining room is a shrine to Kwan Ti, the god of valor. Also on the third floor is a shrine of the Laughing Buddha.

Figures of "the Laughing Buddha" in wood or ceramic may be found in stores in Chinatowns throughout the country, as commonly as are those of Kwan Yin. Seated, his large belly spilling over his lap, the Buddha is laughing gaily. The figure derives from one of the legends of the life of Gautama. Before entering his ministry for six years the young Gautama followed strictly the rules of fasting, self-mortification, and meditation, which marked the retirement from the world of the ascetics of Brahmanism, breaking his fast occasionally with jujube fruits, sesame seeds, and a little rice. "Having only skin and bone remaining, with his fat, flesh, and blood entirely wasted, yet, though diminished, he still shone with undiminished grandeur like the ocean." But it was all to no purpose. It was, he said, "like trying to tie the air in knots . . . True calm is properly obtained by the constant satisfaction of the senses . . . This means is based upon eating food."

Thus he became well fed and joyous, and in this state of being attained perfect enlightenment. It is this event which the figures of the laughing Buddha commemorate.

The new building of the Chinese Benevolent Association has classrooms for a Chinese school and a room for social events as well as a fairly large auditorium. The Ling Long Museum at 2238 S. Wentworth Avenue has an exhibit in diorama form of important events in Chinese history and scenes from Chinese life such as: the invention of Chinese writing, the building of the Great Wall, a funeral, a wedding, and other scenes.

Detroit has a very small Chinatown although the Chinese population is supposed to be about four thousand. The first Chinese to settle in this city is reported to have been Ah Chee who came in 1872. He opened a Chinese restaurant and the population grew slowly. The Chinese community was originally in the Gration and Beaubien section and later moved to Third Avenue around 1920. Today the Chinese inhabitants are spread throughout the city and return to Chinatown only to buy Chinese groceries and to patronize the few Chinese restaurants there.

There are no Chinatowns in the South. The 1960 census shows that there are 16,839 Chinese throughout the Southern states but they are scattered and engaged chiefly in farming and the grocery business. There are some Chinese restaurants in the resort areas of Florida, but not many elsewhere. The South has very few Chinese laundries because washing is generally done at home.

CHAPTER 11

Chinatown, East

New England's contact with China took place before the Chinese started to emigrate to the United States. Its ports, especially Salem, were filled with Oriental goods such as tea and porcelain. The *Empress of China* was the first American ship to return from Canton in May 1785. The cargo which she brought home included silks, teas, nankeens, cassia, and chinaware. In the years that followed until about 1840, teas, textiles, and chinaware led the list of imports from China, and after 1840, silk imports declined because of change in fashion and the demand for chinaware greatly decreased because of the introduction of French and English porcelain in America. And there were, of course, other miscellaneous items in lesser quantities such as sweetmeats, fireworks, lacquerware, grasscloth, fans, matting, shawls, pearl buttons, and Chinese paintings.

"Chinese export porcelain" is the term used for wares specially made in China for foreign markets, particularly the United States. The porcelain was more often than not made to order for the buyer with his monogram, shield, or some special form of decoration. Because these items were personal and had individuality they became family heirlooms and many pieces have been preserved to this day. The porcelain, of course, had a utilitarian purpose and for the middle and lower income groups, China produced large quantities of breakfast, dinner and tea services, many of which were brightly painted. The mating of Eastern and Western cultures produced porcelain with Oriental form, shapes, and craftsmanship with the boldness of American emblems and decorations.

The six major ports in the East were Salem, Boston, Providence, New York, Philadelphia, and Baltimore. There were a few in Connecticut. Some Chinese goods came into such Southern ports as Norfolk, Charleston, Savannah, Mobile and New Orleans.

As California's first contacts with Chinese were with laborers, New England's were with students. A Yung Wing graduated from Yale in 1854. According to Thomas E. LaFargue's *China's First Hundred,* Yung Wing arrived at Monson Academy in Monson, Massachusetts, in 1847, but there is some evidence that as early as 1817 a Chinese was in the foreign mission school in the village of Cornwall, Connecticut, and that at least five Chinese had attended that school at approximately this time. Mr. LaFargue also cites a paper which Dr. William F. Worner read before the Lancaster Historical Society of Pennsylvania on "a Chinese Soldier in the Civil War" in which he relates the experiences of Hong Neok Woo who served in the Pennsylvania militia.

Perhaps New England's first contact with Chinese laborers was with the hundred who were sent to North Adams, Massachusetts, to break a strike in a shoe factory in the 1870s.

The Chinese population in New England today is somewhere between 12,000 and 15,000. The Chinatown which services these people is in Boston. Boston at one time was third in size of Chinese population with San Francisco first and New York second. It now ranks a poor fourth with Los Angeles taking the third place. Once 7000, the estimated Chinese population is 4000 with an additional 2000 to 3000 in the metropolitan Boston area.

Chinatown started in the old Scollay Square district which was dominated primarily by importing firms and small businesses. It was later moved to its present site on

Beach, Tyler, Hudson, Oxford, Harvard, Oak, Kneeland streets, Harrison Avenue and Broadway with Kneeland dividing the business district to the north from the residential district on the south. Fitzgerald Expressway and the Massachusetts Turnpike extension have displaced a number of the Chinese living in the lower-income residential sections. Those who live in Chinatown and who want to stay there are debating the question of building a new settlement. Although fine Chinese restaurants are being built in the suburbs of Boston and all over New England, Boston's Chinatown can still boast some of the best. Boston was where the United States made its early cultural contacts with China and it is said that it was also the place where Dr. Sun Yat-sen met with leaders of a powerful society to plan the overthrow of the Manchu Dynasty, and the establishment of the Republic.

There is little to be said of the Chinese in Philadelphia and Pittsburgh. Philadelphia's Chinatown was greatly reduced in size when the main street of the ghetto was converted into a thoroughfare leading to the Benjamin Franklin Bridge, connecting Philadelphia with Camden, New Jersey. A slum-clearance program further took away some more of Chinatown. The City of Brotherly Love now has 1810 Chinese according to the 1960 census. Pittsburgh's Chinatown was totally obliterated by the building of a modern expressway.

Just when the Chinese discovered New York is not clear, but newspapers of the day indicate that on Saturday, July 10, 1847, thirty-five Chinese arrived at the harbor of New York on the junk *Kee Ying*. James Gordon Bennett's New York *Herald*, as well as the other New York newspapers, reported the event. The New York *Herald* said,

She has had the passage of 212 sailing days from
Canton, having touched at St. Helena, in her arrival has
been looked upon with a good deal of interest. She is
built in a very peculiar style of teakwood, about 150
feet long by 12 feet depth of hold and 25 feet beam.
Her cabin is about 30 feet long, 10½ feet high, and
23 feet wide. Her rudder is suspended by cables made
of bamboo and weighs 7 tons. Anchors are made of
teakwood and the cabin is decorated with representations, or rather paintings, of birds, beasts, etc. An
idol is on board representing a female with 10 pairs of
arms, decorated with flowers, trinkets, beads, etc. We
understand she has a crew of 35 Chinese. Her build and
entire form will be looked upon as a matter of deep
curiosity.

I cannot imagine what the "idol . . . representing a female with 10 pairs of arms," was. It is possible that the
ten pairs of arms were an exaggeration, and that the figure was a representation of either the Hindu Brahma,
or Vishnu, each of whom was commonly represented with
four hands. The fact that both were male deities is not
significant, for their Oriental dress may have made them
seem to be female. In later Hinduism Gautama, Buddha
is believed to have been an incarnation of Vishnu.
Whether this belief ever became a part of Chinese Buddhism (which might have explained the figure) I do not
know, and so the "idol" visitor to New York in 1847 remains a mystery to me, as it was to the New York *Herald* which reported it.

This junk was the object of great curiosity and at the
price of 25 cents per head 50,000 visitors came aboard the
junk, and admired the cleverly made sails, the great eyes
painted on either side of the prow, the wondrous decorations inside the cabin as well as the Chinese crew dressed
in loose cotton jackets, big trousers, small flat caps, and

with long queues. Of great interest also were two Chinese chow dogs with their unusual dark tongues. The junk left New York at the end of August but before it sailed evidently several of the crew jumped ship and started what was to become New York's Chinatown.

During the early 1850s a few Chinese drifted into New York from San Francisco by ship. One of these was Lee Ah Bow, who sailed as a cook of the United States ship called *Valencia,* from San Francisco where he had been in the pea business. The first few Chinese in New York evidently found work as cigar peddlers or sandwich sign carriers. In 1869 a small group traveled to New York overland from the West Coast after working on the railroads. One of these was Chu Fong Wing who helped found New York's Chinese Consolidated Benevolent Association. As the racial tensions on the West Coast heightened and the railroads were completed, larger groups of Chinese came to the East Coast. They settled in the old plow and harrow plot, the site of a seventeenth-century New York farm and tavern west of the Bowery, that takes in Mott, Pell, and Doyer streets.

A Mr. Thomas established a large laundry in Belleville, New Jersey, and hired fifty Chinese to do the labor. On Sundays, their day off, these Chinese laundrymen always visited the old plow and harrow tract to visit friends, buy groceries, clothing, and other necessities. By 1900 there were between 12,000 and 13,000 in and around New York and on Sundays almost all of these could be found in Chinatown, still on the site of the old plow and harrow lot.

Wo Kee opened the first Chinese mercantile establishment in New York about 1875 in Oliver near Cherry Street. The store moved to Park Street and then a short time later to 8 Mott Street where it became the center of Chinatown. Other similar stores opened on Mott Street. They served not only to supply groceries, herbs and Chi-

nese medicines, and other necessities of life but also as
social centers on Sundays where people could gather, pick
up their mail, and chat with their relatives. Many of these
immigrants could neither read nor write Chinese, and so
on Sunday they came to Chinatown to have someone
write home for them and read their mail.

The early immigrants to New York City were generally
young men. Their homes were bachelor quarters near
where they worked. For the hundreds of laundrymen
scattered throughout the metropolitan area, the back
room of the laundry served as home. Here they lived by
themselves and cooked simple meals of rice and a little
meat six days a week. Sunday afforded them the opportunity for eating on a grander style at one of the restaurants in Chinatown. Even in the gaslit days the most decorated and well lit buildings were those occupied by
restaurants. Chinese lanterns with red and gilt trimmings
decorated the balconies. The better restaurants were
found on the second and third floors. The less expensive
restaurants often occupied the basements. They were less
lavishly decorated and usually had sawdust on the floor
and no linen on the table.

Newspapermen from Park Row were probably the first
Caucasians to attempt eating in New York's Chinatown.
It was not until the mid 1890s that Chinese restaurants
welcomed the Caucasian trade. Soon the Chinese restaurant business started to spread throughout the Borough
of Manhattan and into the other boroughs. Today most
restaurants in Chinatown cater to the Caucasian trade,
and they meet serious competition from the hundreds of
restaurants now located in almost every neighborhood in
the metropolitan New York area.

About 25,000 Chinese live in the metropolitan New
York area, of whom about 7000 live in Chinatown. Chinatown is basically five square blocks although the Chinese population has been spreading out to the surround-

ing neighborhoods. Mott Street, named after Joseph
Mott, a butcher and innkeeper, is the main street. The
north boundary is Canal Street which was once a canal
draining collect pond. To the south Chinatown is bounded
by the Bowery, originally called Bouwerie Lane, because
of the bouweries or farms which lined it. To the west
Chinatown is bounded by Mulberry Street, once entirely
an Italian district, but now becoming more and more
a Chinese residential area, although some Italian shops
displaying cheeses and barrels of fish can still be
found.

New York's Chinatown is the supply center of the entire
East Coast for Chinese vegetables, canned goods, and
other important cooking ingredients. The noodle manufacturing companies supply the whole East Coast and
part of the Midwest with the well-known chow mein noodles. Bakeries supply restaurants with almond cookies
and fortune cookies.

Only recently has Chinatown taken on consciously some
of the Oriental motif which identifies it as a Chinatown.
It borrowed the idea of the telephone booths with the
pagoda tops, an Oriental motif, from San Francisco. A
few years ago the On Leong Association at the corner of
Mott and Canal streets erected a large building with a
mixture of Chinese and Western architecture forming a
gateway to Chinatown. More recently the Chinese Community Center on Mott Street has also carried on this
theme of East and West architecture. A debate has been
going on for years as to whether the quarter should be
torn down and rebuilt with such a mixture of Chinese
and Western architecture. The argument on one side is
for better housing conditions and a more attractive and
cleaner Chinatown. On the other hand, many merchants
fear that they may lose their business locations and the
charm which is naturally there. Although no one will
speak out against better housing conditions, there are as

many people for as there are against the Los Angeles type
of Chinatown, which is built purely for commercial reasons.

But even without the Oriental architecture there is no
mistaking that this is Chinatown. Chinese people young
and old are found milling around the streets running to
and fro although only some of the Chinese women wear
traditional clothing. Chinese men are almost always
dressed in business suits. Windows of grocery stores display many varieties of unusual Chinese vegetables. If
you look hard enough at some of the dimly lit store windows you may find the Chinese apothecary shops carrying dried sea horses, deer antlers, and other Chinese
herbs. Large wooden signs protrude from the walls of the
building with gilded Chinese characters. Very often these
are the names of the family and village associations.

Looking down Mott Street from Canal, one is struck
by the many neon signs standing as tall as five and six
stories high advertising restaurants on this well-lit street.
There are about sixty eating establishments in these five
square blocks. A closer look at some of these buildings
will show the visitor that this is a street where the ground
floors and basements are used for business establishments
and tenements occupy the rest of the building.

The tourist guides attempt to paint Chinatown as a
mysterious and dangerous place to visit in order to add
a thrill for their customers. Nothing could be further from
the truth. Chinatown is one of the safest areas in New
York City.

CHAPTER 12

Retrospect and Prospect

The Chinese in America have been patronized, welcomed, lynched, despised, excluded, hated, liked, admired, but rarely understood or simply accepted. They have been creatures of whom stereotypes have been created. They have been pictured as wise, crafty, honest, frugal, law-abiding, soulless. We all know that "a Chinaman's chance" means no chance at all. Most adults today might still remember the rhyme:

Chink, Chink, Chinaman sitting on a rail,
Along came a white man and cut off his tail.

That is, fortunately, a couplet of a bygone day. We almost never hear "Chink" used any more and most people know that "Chinaman" has a derogatory connotation because of the reference to "John Chinaman," implying that Chinese were all alike and had no individuality.

From the time of the Exclusion Act of 1882 (discussed in Chapter 3) until its repeal in 1943 the Chinese population remained under 100,000. The racial prejudice which brought about the Exclusion Act and its renewal in 1892 continued strongly into the early part of the twentieth century.

In the Act of 1924 Congress imposed a bar on other Asiatics including the Japanese, the agitation against whom had begun in 1900. In 1890 there were only 2039 Japanese and between 1901 and 1910, 132,706 were admitted to the United States. Under the Chinese Exclusion Act of 1882, the alien Chinese wife of a United States citizen was admissible to the country. Under the Act of 1924 she was excluded because she was ineligible for citizenship.

By the 1920s the Chinese had removed themselves from the competitive labor markets and concentrated in laundries, restaurants, and grocery stores. The mah jong craze came into full swing and so did the elaborate Chinese restaurants which offered dancing and entertainment during prohibition. The Chinese were no longer despised; they were looked upon as oddities in a day where the offbeat was in fashion. The evil and inscrutable stereotype remained as Hollywood produced a popular series of Dr. Fu Manchu movies. In the 1930s the film portrayal changed to Charlie Chan, a "damned clever Chinese." At least he was on the side of the law.

Throughout the period of Chinese immigration, American missionaries went to China first by the hundreds, then by the thousands. By 1931 the young Republic of China was engaged in the Sino-Japanese War. The missionary groups in America late in the thirties started an intensive campaign to boycott Japanese goods, stop shipment of arms and supplies to Japan and tell of the heroism of the Chinese and the brutality of the Japanese.

The tide was turning. With Hitler chewing up Europe, Spain in a civil war, and Japan running through a paper giant, the American public, though isolationist, started to show sympathy for the underdogs. After Pearl Harbor we were clearly allies. Since the strategy of the allies was to concentrate first on the European battle, the picture of the Chinese warriors as presented in the press was that of glamorous heroes with limited supplies and trained soldiers. War-time movies such as *The Flying Tigers, God Is My Co-Pilot, China Girl,* among others, gave millions of American people this impression.

In 1943 President Roosevelt asked Congress to repeal the Chinese Exclusion Act, and during the same year

Madame Chiang Kai-shek, a graduate of Wellesley College in Massachusetts, beautiful and articulate, came to the United States to plead for aid to China. Not only was she a fantastic success with the public, but after her speech before Congress, as *Time* magazine put it, "tough guys" melted.

This was nearly a century after the arrival of the first Chinese laborers. Never before and never again have the Chinese stood on such a high pedestal. It did not last long, however. The over glamorous picture became a disillusionment. The corruption in Chiang's government became apparent. Soon after the end of the Second World War, the hero crumbled and within a few years we were fighting one China and supporting another.

The two-China situation has caused the Chinese in America, particularly the first generation, to take stock of themselves. They have been cut off from their ancestral homeland. They can identify neither with the Communist nor the Nationalist governments. In effect the umbilical cord of the *gum san hok*—the sojourner—has been cut. He had been deceiving himself into thinking that he was merely a "Gold Mountain guest." In fact, few of them after the turn of the nineteenth century actually did return to China. Some of them visited their homes occasionally, generally every five years or so. With few exceptions they remitted a large part of their income to the family at home until the Communists took over. Then even this became impossible.

When the Exclusion Act was finally repealed in 1943, the Chinese were given an annual quota of only 105 immigrants per year. Although the immigration laws are still discriminatory against the Chinese, several laws have permitted them to bring their wives and children to America. After World War II Congress passed the War Brides Act of 1945 which allowed war brides and children to enter the United States as non-quota immigrants. The number of Chinese wives admitted during the eight years that followed were: 1946, 159; 1947, 902; 1948, 3192; 1949, 2143; 1950, 1062; 1951, 826; 1952, 4220; 1953, 2042. Not all of these were GI brides but it can be assumed that most of them were.

The Refugee Relief Act of 1953 admitted 2000 Chinese and 300 Far Eastern refugees.

These more liberal immigration acts will have a profound effect on the Chinese community in America.

Because it was at first financially difficult and later for some time legally impossible to bring one's wife to America, the ratio of male to female has been disproportionate. At the peak of Chinese immigration in 1890, when there were 107,488 Chinese in America, there was a ratio of 100 females to 2678 males. In 1920 when the Chinese population was only 61,639, the ratio was 695 males to 100 females. The liberalization of immigration laws allowing wives and children into the United States has changed the ratio. It now stands at 100 females to 133 males. The census of 1960 shows 237,292 Chinese in America.

Chinatown, U.S.A., has not only grown in size, it has changed in character. The "bachelor" sojourner, who after many years of separation brought over his wife and children, has become a family man, and his attitude toward his community, its schools, safety, cleanliness, even tongs have changed. For about a hundred years a large majority of the Chinese in America lived unnatural lives away from their wives and children. Their contribution in terms of service was by no means small but their total orientation was toward their homeland. Thus, they cared little about their communities here. The reuniting of the Chinese family in America has therefore changed the outlook of the sojourner. He can now be expected to take part in and be concerned with problems which are confronted by any family man in America. He will, however, have problems which other Americans do not have.

If his children are in their teens or older when they arrive, the chances are that their adjustment will be difficult. Unless they can learn English quickly and catch up with their education, they must enter a Chinese business. If the children have been born in this country, then it is the parent who must go through the adjustment which accompanies bringing up an American child. No matter how hard parents try, their children are, by and large, Chinese only in looks, particularly those who are third or fourth generation. They cannot read or write Chinese, and can barely speak it. The desire to conform and be like everyone else, meaning the Americans, even in Chinatown, is too great to be suppressed.

It is said that the Chinese have the greatest respect for scholarship and therefore would sacrifice anything for their children's education. This does not apply to the sojourners who came from the villages of China. Although they theoretically valued education, their feeling for China was such that they did not fully accept American schooling. There is hardly a second-generation Chinese-American who has not had to work to help pay his tuition if he has gone to college. Usually he has attended state or city supported schools. Until recently, it was rare for him "to go away" to college. The idea of his leaving home seemed to his parents to indicate the imminence of his total Americanization, something which the sojourners abhorred. Many who had been accepted by Ivy League schools have not been able to go because of family objection or family refusal to pay the tuition. The objections were not based on money alone which was sometimes justified but also on the statement that "one school is as good as another." The enrollment of a sojourner's child in one of the fine prep schools such as Groton, Exeter, and the like is still considered a great waste of money.

Until World War II Chinese girls were usually discouraged from going to college, even state and city supported institutions.

The dream of the sojourner was that his son would eventually take over his established business and remit moneys to China when he retired there. Of course, there were exceptions, forward-looking parents who encouraged their children to enter the professions. In such cases, medicine was usually preferred and after that law and engineering.

It is ironic that it took a Communist conquest of mainland China to bring about a healthy change in attitude of the sojourners in America. Without the hope of retirement in China, or the relocation of their family there (which seldom happened anyway) the sojourners are devoting themselves to finding happiness and fulfillment in America. This effect will be greatly felt by their children in the changed attitude toward education and acculturation. It is felt also by the older group's willingness to use savings put aside for retirement, on things such as homes, new clothes, cars, and television sets. Although we sometimes decry the materialism in America, the sojourner has been so frugal that it has affected his whole orientation to life, deferring happiness and pleasure for that unknown time when he can retire. If the Chinese experience in Arizona is any example, the Chinese families will Americanize rapidly.

In my trip around the country, I found Chinese, especially those in Tucson and Phoenix, Arizona, some of them men in their sixties and born in China, who spoke grammatically correct English without a Chinese accent. Many of them live in nice middle-class homes in American neighborhoods, and their children are being brought up with American attitudes. They favor higher education and advancement in America. They understand that the retention of Chinese culture by their children is an up-hill battle, though they keep trying.

Several factors have prevented or inhibited the Chinese immigrants as a group from marrying Caucasian women. Twenty-nine states have or have had at one time or another laws prohibiting or discouraging mixed marriages; Georgia (1927) and Virginia (1930) passed acts requiring racial data about forebears. In South Carolina, a white man may marry a Chinese woman, but not vice versa. California's act was not abolished until 1948. A criminal statute in Mississippi prohibits the publication or circulation of printed matter favoring interracial marriage. The second factor is that most of the immigrants were married men.

Finally, the Chinese families frown on mixed marriages. This strong attitude based on the feeling that the Chinese race is superior to other races applies as well to marriage with other Orientals such as Japanese, Korean, Indonesian, etc., although this is usually rationalized by the argument that the non-Chinese are not familiar with the Chinese language and customs. The Chinese parents from Kwangtung Province oppose marriages with Chinese of other provinces because they speak a different dialect and have different customs. The fact that their second generation children do not speak Chinese or know about Chinese customs has no influence on this irrational prejudice. In this respect, the people from Kwangtung are extremely provincial. Of course, most white families also oppose interracial marriage which they consider to be mongrelization. There are mixed marriages in Hawaii, but the experience there is not characteristic of the behavior on the mainland of the U.S.A. Many of the early emigrants to Hawaii were not Cantonese but Hakka, who were a seafaring people less concerned with customs.

The low incidence of juvenile delinquency in Chinatown has attracted more attention in national magazines and newspapers than any other aspect of Chinese life in America. This happy situation is undoubtedly due to the strongly knit family unity evident in first and somewhat in the second-generation Chinese homes. The accepted authority of the father and the ingrained attitude of respect for one's elders creates a respect for authority outside, as well as within, the home. This is probably the main element for the low rate of juvenile delinquency.

Other influences, such as family associations, have been played up by magazines, but I do not consider these arguments valid. It is argued that a child is hesitant to do any wrong because his misdeed would bring "loss of face" to his whole family or village clan. I doubt very much whether a would-be juvenile delinquent ever thinks of his act affecting the hundreds of clan members, some of whom he does not even know. However, the family association does have an indirect effect. Chinatown is geographically a small place of several blocks, very much like a small town, and it is impossible to do anything wrong without someone who knows your family finding out about it. The social pressure of any town that small would have a greater effect on behavior.

But it is evident that as parents tend to show less interest and control over the home, a social behavior will take place. Since World War II, many of the mothers have been working during the day and the family unit has not been as closely knit. San Francisco and New York have recently been concerned with teenage gangs. Some of these gangs are composed of China-born youth who are frustrated by their inability to do anything except work in restaurants or laundries. Children of families which moved away from Chinatown are brought up as are any other American children. Third, fourth, and fifth-generation Chinese-Americans can be expected to be as good and as bad as any other American children. They will make major contributions in the professions. Many have done so already.

Senator Hiram L. Fong of Hawaii was the first person of Oriental ancestry to be nominated for President of the United States. His nomination as "favorite son" candidate at the Republican National Convention in San Francisco in 1964, even though it did not receive much attention in the press, was covered by television, putting the American public on notice that the image of the Chinese in America is changing. Senator Fong, son of a sugar plantation laborer, is a successful businessman and attorney who received a bachelor's degree from the University of Hawaii and his law degree from Harvard. After his election to the U. S. Senate, honorary degrees were conferred on him by Tufts University and Lafayette College.

Chinese have been in American politics not only in Hawaii where the population is primarily Oriental. Chinese legislators have served in the state assemblies of Arizona and Florida as well as the city councils of Seattle and Phoenix. Chinese judges include the Honorable Delbert Wong of California and Honorable Thomas Tang of Phoenix, Arizona.

International recognition was given to two China-born scientists in their early thirties who received the Nobel Prize in 1957. Professors Tsung Dao Lee and Chen-Ning Yang of Columbia University and the Institute for Advance Study at Princeton shattered what was considered a fundamental law of physics called the principle of the conservation of parity. Many of the discussions leading to this great discovery took place in small Chinese restaurants where the two theoretical physicists conferred. The 1957 Albert Einstein Award in Science cited Dr. Lee and Dr. Yang "for bringing about a development of profound importance in the search for understanding of the elementary particles of which the universe is constituted."

The theories which Dr. Lee and Dr. Yang introduced

were proved correct in experiments by a Chinese woman, Dr. Chien-Shiung Wu, and a team of specialists at the National Bureau of Standards. Dr. Wu who is professor of physics at Columbia University is widely recognized as one of the leading experimental physicists in the world. At home, she is a wife and mother, her husband being also a well-known physicist of the Brookhaven National Laboratory.

The list of Chinese making significant and important contributions in science is long and we can mention only a few. Dr. Kuan H. Sun has been manager of the Westinghouse radiation and nucleonics laboratory since 1955. The isolation of five of the six major pituitary hormones was accomplished under the direction of Dr. Cho-Hao Li, a professor of biochemistry and a director of the Hormone Research Laboratory. An organism was named *Nyctotherus cheni* after a Chinese biologist Dr. Tse-Tuan Chen who discovered this new species of protozoa. Dr. Chen is a full professor in biology at the University of Southern California.

The leading research pharmacologist of Eli Lilly Company is Ko-Kwei Chen who has been with the company since 1929.

For some reason, a great number of Chinese have entered the engineering profession. The dean of the college of engineering at Detroit Institute of Technology is Dr. A. T. Lui who received his college education in China and earned his doctorate at the University of Michigan. Chinese engineers have played a major role in the space age making significant contributions in the development of the Megawatt Klystron, microwave aerials, electronic computer systems, microwave tubes, electrical propulsion systems, high-energy propellant combustion, jet propulsion, rocket combustion, and in many other areas of technical research. Chinese engineers are professors at universities throughout the country.

A number have entered the field of architecture and the one who is known internationally is I. M. Pei.

The number of Chinese scholars in the social sciences is smaller than the number in the pure sciences or engineering. Fifty-three Chinese scholars are listed in *American Men of Science*. Of those who are teaching in universities, most of them are working in Far Eastern departments. The subject which claims the largest number is economics. A Chinese-American, Dr. Rose Hum Lee, headed the department of sociology at Roosevelt College in Chicago.

Lin Yutang who has written many books including his *Importance of Living* (1937) is probably the best known Chinese author in America. His books have wide and popular readership. *The Flower Drum Song* written by C. Y. Lee was made into a Broadway musical and later a movie by Rodgers and Hammerstein. The book, his first novel, was a story about life in San Francisco's Chinatown. Shortly thereafter, *Lover's Point* was published. He is now a Hollywood film writer. Chiang Yee, a distinguished Chinese artist, author, and poet, has written a number of books on various subjects. Diana Chang is a respected novelist. Her father was born in China and is a successful architect. She is married to a Caucasian and is now Mrs. David Herrmann.

In the arts there is Dong Kingman who has won wide acclaim as an artist, not just for Chinese themes but also for scenes of America. His watercolors have been reproduced in such national magazines as *Life, Holiday,* and *Fortune*. James Wong Howe, known for many years in Hollywood for his sensitive photography, won an Oscar for photography in *The Rose Tattoo* in 1957. Chinese musicians are still not well known. A Chinese, Wen-Chung Chou, had his works performed by the San Francisco Symphony Orchestra under the baton of Leopold Stokowski and was the first Chinese composer to receive a Guggenheim fellowship. His style includes the marriage of

Western music with classical Chinese. In the classical opera, Yi Kwei-sze, a bass-baritone, has appeared on television in Mozart's *Magic Flute* and has given recitals throughout the country.

The Chinese in America who have sought success have achieved it in spite of their racial background. Being Chinese is seldom an advantage in the professional world. Except for the race riots early in California, anti-Chinese prejudice has been generally subtle and seldom as strong as the prejudice against Jews and certainly infinitely less than that against the Negroes.

During the Korean War, many Chinese-Americans experienced unpleasantness because they were considered the "enemy." Many have wondered what the attitude will be when the two-China policy is abandoned and only Communist China remains. These people have not forgotten the horrible Japanese relocation camps on the West Coast during the Second World War.

The Chinese-Americans are experiencing fewer barriers in education, social life, and occupational opportunities. But irritating reminders appear from time to time particularly in housing. Nationwide attention was given to an incident in 1952 in Southwood, South San Francisco, where a meeting of townspeople voted against selling a house to Mr. Sing Sheng who had already made a down payment. The New York *Times* in 1959 carried an article about an assistant professor of geography at Catholic University in Washington, Dr. Chiao-min Hsieh, who with his family was denied admittance at two Maryland beaches because they were not Caucasians. Dr. Hsieh had also been former director of research projects for the office of Naval Research at the Massachusetts Institute of Technology.

These reminders of racial discrimination rarely appear in the newspapers. Usually they arise in employment practices of smaller American corporations or in smaller cities. The complaint is often heard that promotion to positions of responsibility and executive titles comes only if the Chinese is head and shoulders over the Caucasian competitors for the same position. Some Chinese-Americans have thought that the problem could be solved by burying their heritage.

The problem which faces each second-generation Chinese-American but less so for each succeeding generation is what is called "cultural conflict." The first generation or sojourners had established their Chinese attitudes, behavior patterns and norms, and transplanted them here in their Chinatowns. What each succeeding generation experiences is a process of acculturation and assimilation which can be painful. The demands of the outside society to conform to American ways and of the Chinese society to retain his cultural heritage brings about conflicts in everyday matters such as discipline, dating, and schooling.

As the Chinese-American loses his ability to speak Chinese fluently he becomes unable to discuss his ambitions and hopes with his parents. The conflict subsides as he establishes himself in his work and as the older parents realize that there is no hope of returning to China. It is then realized that the old-world ways are not sufficient for survival in America but foreign-born parents and grandparents still believe that Chinese mores and values based on Confucian ethics are superior to Western mores and values. And perhaps they are right.

Most people won't admit it but many children are ashamed of their foreign-born parents. So long as they were attending schools near Chinatown the differences of their parents were less noticeable. But as they went into another neighborhood or on to college, they were embarrassed by the poor English which their parents spoke and their old-world ways. They were ashamed of their homes in back of the laundry, or above the store, and seldom invited their Caucasian friends to visit. Homes of foreign-born parents are generally modestly furnished and cramped for space. They usually do not have special chinaware for company as might be found in American homes. Luxuries are few, each item purchased being utilitarian. The purchase of television sets takes a great deal of begging and hi-fi sets and record collections are rare in such homes.

The Chinese-American children of parents living in Chinatown rarely experience a common family outing such as going to a picnic, or to a ballgame or even to a circus. Generally if they live in Chinatown, the father has to work on weekends when business with tourists is good and consequently there is little time when school holidays coincide with his days off. If the parents are laundrymen, Sundays are spent in Chinatown visiting relatives and purchasing food supplies for the week.

If these Chinese-Americans ever thought about it, they would see that they had not been cheated. Although they did not know the comradery of "togetherness" outside the home which their Caucasian classmates experienced and which the magazines write about, they nevertheless received a great deal of love and devotion from their parents. To be sure the love was not demonstrative or outward, but it was strong.

The conflict between the foreign-born parent and his Chinese-American children has centered on the parent's sojourner attitude. So long as the parent thought that he and his family would some day return to China to live in luxury, he resisted, and he wanted his children to resist, American ways. The sojourner attitude has been dying out rapidly.

Outside of Chinatown, living in the suburbs or other parts of the city, the second, third, and fourth generation Chinese-Americans are being assimilated into middle-class American society as engineers, scientists, doctors, dentists, lawyers, and businessmen. It is often assumed that Chinese-Americans are culturally Chinese. At best you can say that they know that they are of Chinese ancestry.

The Chinese-American who thinks that he can bury his Chinese heritage deceives himself. He need only look in a mirror to remind himself that he is physically a Chinese and will always be identified as such, at least at first meeting.

There will be an eventual assimilation and acculturation of the Chinese into American society. The more liberal immigration laws allowing wives and children to enter the United States have had an effect on the Chinese community making it a more natural family oriented community. With their families here and no homeland to return to, the emphasis will be on accomplishments in this country rather than on one thousands of miles away.

Chinatown will eventually die away except for New York and San Francisco where new immigrants will always start. The suburbanization of America has caused a recession of business for almost all of the Chinatowns in America. Most of them are located in poor, deteriorated sections of town where parking of cars is difficult. Many Chinese restaurants therefore have also moved out to the suburbs. Families will move out in order to be closer to work and to get away from the poor housing conditions of Chinatown. Chinatown will become, for the Chinese, a place to purchase Chinese goods and groceries. It will remain as a ghetto only to the extent that the tourist trade continues to patronize it and new immigrants arrive to sustain it.

What has prevented assimilation has been caused as much by the Chinese's own aloofness as by his difference in language and custom. This will gradually disappear but what will remain will be his physical differences.

Bibliography

Asbury, Herbert, *The Barbary Coast*, Alfred Knopf, New York, 1933.

Bancroft, H. H., *History of California, 1860–1890*, Bancroft and Company, San Francisco, 1895.

Bode, William, *Lights and Shadows of Chinatown*, H. S. Crocker Company, San Francisco, 1896.

Borthwick, J. D., *Three Years in California*, William Blackwood and Sons, Edinburgh, MDCCC LVIII.

Bromley, Isaac H., *The Chinese Massacre at Rock Springs Wyoming*, Franklin Press: Rand Avery and Company, 1886.

Brown, Donald, *China Trade Days in California*, University of California Press, Berkeley, 1947.

Burkhardt, V. R., *Chinese Creeds and Customs, Vol. II*, The South China Morning Post, Ltd., Hong Kong, 1955.

Buxton, L. H. D., *China the Land and the People*, Clarendon Press, Oxford, 1929.

Chan, Wing-Tsit, *Religious Trends in Modern China*, Columbia University Press, New York, 1953.

Chang, M., *Tides from the West*, Yale University Press, New Haven, 1947.

Chapman, C. E., *A History of California: the Spanish Period*, The Macmillan Company, New York, 1920.

Cheng, F. T., *Musings of a Chinese Gourmet*, Hutchinson, London, 1954.

Coolidge, M., *Chinese Immigration*, Henry Holt, New York, 1909.

Creel, H. G., *Chinese Thought*, Menton Book, New York, 1953.

Creel, H. G., *Confucius and the Chinese Way*, Harper & Brothers, New York, 1949.

Creel, H. G., *Confucius: the Man and the Myth*, John Day Company, New York, 1949.

Crow, Carl, *Four Hundred Million Customers*, Hamish Hamilton, London, 1937.

deBary, W. T., *Sources of Chinese Tradition*, Columbia University Press, New York, 1960.

Dillon, Richard H., *The Hatchet Men*, Coward-McCann, Inc., New York, 1962.

Dobie, Charles C., *San Francisco's Chinatown*, D. Appleton-Century Company, New York, 1936.

Eberhard, Wolfram, *Chinese Festivals*, Henry Schuman, New York, 1952.

Elegant, Robert S., *The Dragon's Seed*, St. Martin's Press, New York, 1959.

Fairbank, John K., *The United States and China* (rev. ed.) Harvard University Press, Cambridge, 1958.

Ferguson, John Calvin, *Chinese Mythology*, Cooper Square Publishers, New York, 1964.

Fung Yu-lan, *A Short History of Chinese Philosophy*, The Macmillan Company, 1950.

Genthe, Arnold and Will Irwin, *Old Chinatown*, Mitchell Kennerly, New York, 1913.

Gibson, Otis, *The Chinese in America*, Hitchcock and Walden, Cincinnati, 1877.

Glazer, Nathan, *The Integration of American Immigrants*, Law and Contemporary Problems, 21 (Spr. 1956): 256–269.

Glick, Carl, *Double Ten*, McGraw-Hill, New York, 1945.

Glick, Carl, *Shake Hands with the Dragon*, McGraw-Hill, New York, 1945.

Glick, Carl, *Three Time I Bow*, Whittlesley House, New York, 1943.

Glick, Carl and Hong Sheng-hwa, *Swords of Silence: Chinese Secret Societies*, Past and Present, Whittlesley House, New York, 1947.

Groot, Jan, *The Religious System of China*, Published with a subvention from Dutch colonial govt. . . . Leyden, E. J. Brill, 1892–1910.

Groussett, René, *The Rise and Splendor of the Chinese Empire*, University of California Press, 1958.

Gulick, Sidney, *American Democracy and Asiatic Citizenship*, Charles Scribner's Sons, New York, 1918.

Hibbert, E. T., *Jesuit Adventure in China During the Reign of Kang Hsi*, E. P. DuHon & Co., New York, 1941.

Hodous, Lewis, *Folkways in China*, A. Probsthain, London, 1929.

Hsu, Francis L. K., *Americans and Chinese: Two Ways of Life*, Henry Schumann, New York, 1953.

Hsu, Francis L. K., *Under the Ancestor's Shadow*, Routledge and Kegan Paul, London, 1949.

Issacs, H. R., *Scratches on Our Minds*, John Day, New York, 1958.

Jackson, Joseph H., *Anybody's Gold*, D. Appleton-Century Company, 1941.

Konvitz, M. R., *The Alien and the Asiatic in American Law*, Cornell University Press, Ithaca, 1946.

Kung, S. S., *Chinese in American Life*, University of Washington Press, Seattle, 1962.

LaFargue, Thomas E., *China's First Hundred*, State College of Washington, Pullman, 1942.

Lang, Olga, *Chinese Family and Society*, Yale University Press, New Haven, 1946.

Latourette, K. S., *The Chinese: Their History and Culture*, The Macmillan Company, New York, 1947.

Lee, Calvin, *Chinese Cooking for American Kitchens*, G. P. Putnam's Sons, New York, 1959.

Lee, Rose Hum, *The Chinese in the United States of America*, Hong Kong University Press, 1960.

Leong, Gor Yum, *Chinatown Inside Out*, B. Bussey, New York, 1936.

Lewis, Oscar, *The Big Four*, Alfred A. Knopf, New York, 1938.

Lowe, Pardee, *Father and Glorious Descendant*, Little, Brown, Boston, 1943.

Lin, Yutang, *My Country and My People*, John Day Company, New York, 1935.

McKenzie, R. D., *Oriental Exclusion*, University of Chicago Press, 1927.

McLeod, Alexander, *Pigtails and Gold Dust,* The Caxton Printers, Caldwell, Idaho, 1947.

Meany, E. S., *History of the State of Washington,* The Macmillan Company, New York, 1909.

Mears, E. G., *Resident Orientals on the American Pacific Coast: Their Legal and Economic Status,* University of Chicago Press, Chicago, 1928.

Myrdal, Gunnar, *The American Dilemma,* Harper & Brothers, New York, 1944.

Palmer, Albert W., *Orientals in American Life,* Friendship Press, New York, 1934.

Reichelt, Karl, *Religion in Chinese Garment,* Lutterworth Press, London, 1951.

Reichwein, Adolf, *China and Europe,* K. Paul Trench, Trubner & Co. Ltd., London, 1925.

Rowbotham, Arnold, *Missionary and Mandarin, the Jesuits at the Court of China,* University of California Press, Berkeley and Los Angeles, 1942.

San Francisco *Alta California,* files.

San Francisco *Argonaut,* files.

San Francisco *Bulletin,* files.

San Francisco *Chronicle,* files.

San Francisco *Examiner,* files.

San Francisco *Herald,* files.

Seward, George F., *Chinese Immigration in its Social and Economic Aspects,* Charles Scribner's Sons, New York, 1881.

Smith, W. C., "Changing Personality Traits of Second Generation Orientals of America," *American Journal of Sociology* 33 (1928): 922–929.

Speer, William, *China and California,* Marvin and Hitchcock, San Francisco, 1853.

Townsend, L. T., *The Chinese Problem,* Lee and Shepard, Boston, 1876.

Wilkinson, Hiram P., *The Family in Classical China,* Kelly & Walsh, Ltd., Shanghai, 1926.

Williams, G. W., *Chinese Immigration,* Charles Scribner's Sons, New York, 1912.

Wilson, Carol G., *Chinatown Quest,* Stanford University Press, Stanford, California, 1950.

Winfield, Gerald F., *China: The Land and the People*, William
Sloane Associates, Inc., New York, 1948.

Wong, Jade Snow, *Fifth Chinese Daughter*, Harper & Brothers,
New York, 1950.

Index